# PHYSICIAN ASSISTED SUICIDE

The *Special Topics in Health and Faith Series* also includes:

Religion and Public Discourse:
Principles and Guidelines for Religious Participants

The Challenges of Aging:
Retrieving Spiritual Traditions

# PHYSICIAN ASSISTED SUICIDE
## Religious and Public Policy Perspectives

◆

Edwin R. DuBose

Published by

THE PARK RIDGE CENTER
FOR THE STUDY OF HEALTH, FAITH, AND ETHICS
211 E. Ontario · Suite 800 · Chicago, Illinois · 60611-3215

PHYSICIAN ASSISTED SUICIDE
Religious and Public Policy Perspectives

Edwin R. DuBose

Cover artwork courtesy of the Estate of Ana Mendieta
From the series *Body Tracks (Rastros Corporales), 1982*
by Ana Mendieta
Blood and tempera paint on paper.

Rose Art Museum, Brandeis University, Waltham, Massachusetts;
Rose Purchase Fund, 1991

Photo: Dan Soper

Book design: Haru Furuya

©1999 by The Park Ridge Center for the Study of Health, Faith, and Ethics

Published by
    The Park Ridge Center
    for the Study of Health, Faith, and Ethics
    211 East Ontario Street, Suite 800
    Chicago, Illinois 60611

ISBN: 0-945482-00-0
Ethics/Medical/Legal/Religion

Printed in Canada

# CONTENTS

# FOREWORD

The complex issues surrounding physician-assisted suicide frequently leave legislators, as well as those they represent, bewildered, confused, frustrated, and even angry.

This handbook provides those interested in public policy with a brief yet comprehensive overview of the debate about physician-assisted suicide (PAS), paying particular attention to the views of religious traditions in the United States. A number of initiatives supported by policy groups as well as legislators are under way in various states to improve end-of-life care short of assisted suicide—initiatives such as state laws affecting pain management, advance directives, and the regulation and financing of those who provide care to dying patients. In June 1997, however, the U. S. Supreme Court affirmed that state legislatures also may decide whether to legalize physician-assisted suicide. As a result, state legislators across the country are considering bills pertaining to PAS. As one of the most troubling issues to arise in medicine for many years, physician-assisted suicide threatens to be as contentious as the abortion issue.

One factor policy makers will weigh in making their decisions about assisted suicide is the religious voice, a source of strongly held views on the subject of suicide, suffering, compassion, and the value of life and its ultimate purpose. Unfortunately, in most of the debate over physician-assisted suicide, the media presents a one-sided portrayal of the religious perspective. Focusing on strident religious opposition to legalizing assisted suicide, the media often fails to depict the diverse views held by people of faith. While many religious people give thoughtful and coherent reasons to oppose physician-assisted suicide, a number support legalization. Since the complex questions raised by PAS touch on some of the deepest of human values, a careful policy analysis requires a fair and objective review of the concerns raised about physician-assisted suicide.

In producing this handbook, the Park Ridge Center's research staff has tried to be succinct, objective, and informative. Wherever possible, we refer to official statements by each religious denomination's governing or other formal body or allude to positions formulated by authorities within that tradition. In any religious tradition, however, there may be more than one denomination, groups that stress different emphases, or sects that maintain views in opposition to mainstream positions. The groups treated here were selected on the basis of membership size and degree of centralization or organization. In citing statements or positions espoused by particular bodies within a tradition, we recognize that the positions of other groups may not be represented, especially those with smaller memberships and those with greater nonconformist or independent tendencies. We have made every effort to be precise and fair within the limits of our resources and the cooperation of representatives of the various religious groups.

We also recognize that the beliefs and values of individuals within a tradition may vary from the so-called "official" position of their tradition. One's understanding of his or her tradition's beliefs or one's acceptance of a particular position is likely to be modified by many factors. In fact, some traditions leave moral decisions about these issues to individual conscience. We therefore caution the reader against generalizing too readily from statements about the tradition to the individual believer's particular position.

The Park Ridge Center does not advocate a particular position on physician-assisted suicide. Rather, our intent is to enhance informed policy debate and decision-making by providing a fair and objective review of various religious traditions' perspectives. In the years ahead, many policy leaders will have to make complex ethical decisions on this issue, and such leaders have an opportunity to effect change that will have a profound impact on millions of Americans' lives and deaths.

# CHAPTER | ONE

# PERSONAL NARRATIVES

■ □ □

The questions and potential problems associated with physician-assisted suicide arise in the daily struggles of many terminally ill and severely debilitated persons and their families. Because of the pain and suffering of their medical condition or because of the fear of a possible future medical condition, many feel that PAS should be an option for them. In order to present the question of assisted suicide as it usually arises—out of people's experiences—we will begin this discussion with four stories: a young man with AIDS, a middle-aged mother with Alzheimer's disease, another with leukemia, and an elderly woman who has suffered a stroke.

✢ ✢ ✢

## Steve

After living almost ten years with an AIDS diagnosis, Steve now felt that his illness had the upper hand. Cytomegalovirus retinitis impaired his vision, and he showed more serious indications of AIDS dementia complex, particularly periods of temporary confusion and loss of memory. While still capable of decision-making—and at the urging of Mark, a physician friend—he completed a living will specifying that no resuscitative efforts be made. Determined to fight as long as he could, Steve tried to maintain an optimistic outlook, although his phone calls to family and friends began to take on a tone of finality.

Recently discharged from the hospital after another bout of pneumonia, Steve suddenly declared his desire to die at home, surrounded by the people who meant so much to him. He did not want another hospitalization, and after lengthy discussion, he and his lover felt comfortable with the decision. Steve did not share his thoughts with his mother, who wanted him to continue aggressive medical care as long as it would prolong his life. Not wanting his deteriorating condition to lead to what he perceived as a death without dignity, Steve asked his primary-care physician to assist his death with an overdose of medication. When his physician had qualms about complying with this request, Steve turned to his physician friend Mark to help him when the time came. Steve began to plan for his funeral.

Extremely weak from his illness and in great pain, Steve remained bedridden and dependent upon his caregivers for almost everything. As a result of his brain infection, he had weakness on his right side and an involuntary tremor. Chronic viral and protozoan infections in his bowel caused unrelenting diarrhea. He experienced vision problems and received a morphine drip with a push every two hours for the pain. Finally, Steve developed a cough and fever. Having been through this before, he suspected that he had another lung infection. After tossing all night in pain and discomfort, Steve told Mark that it was time to die.

## Janet

Married for thirty-three years, with three sons in their twenties, Janet was a bright, funny, and intelligent woman who read philosophy, politics, and much of the literature on death and dying. She taught English at a community college and piano lessons at home, and she and her husband were members of the Unitarian Church. Sometime in 1986, while sight-reading piano music, Janet began to falter. At first she thought she needed glasses, but after a physical exam, her doctor diagnosed her with the early stages of Alzheimer's disease (Webb 1997).

Janet and her husband had had long conversations about their preferences for a "death with dignity" if they ever found themselves terminally ill and incapacitated. Now she thought about how she would die while she was still coherent enough to make a plan and decided she did not want to undergo the sustained mental deterioration that Alzheimer's would involve: loss of memory, confusion, increasing inability to recognize others, and, finally, a loss of all cognitive function.

In September 1989, while looking through *Newsweek* magazine, Janet read about Jack Kevorkian and his "suicide machine." Her husband contacted Kevorkian, who requested her medical records, consulted with her physicians, and talked with Janet and her husband several times about their wishes. After a three-month experimental drug treatment for Alzheimer's, Janet decided to call Kevorkian again. Because of the legal stipulations on end-of-life care, Kevorkian insisted that Janet make her choices clear while she was still "legally competent." In June 1990, following extensive conversations with their sons, minister, and doctor, Janet and her husband flew to Michigan and said their good-byes. After Kevorkian inserted an intravenous line into her arm, Janet pushed a lever on the device that first delivered saline solution, then the sedative thiopental, and finally potassium chloride to stop her heart. She became Kevorkian's first assisted suicide, dying in the back of his van.

## Diane

Diane went to her doctor complaining of fatigue and a rash. Her physician conducted several tests, including checking her blood count, and the results caused him to suspect leukemia. Concerned, he suggested to Diane that the tests be repeated, and when she pressed him for possibilities, he reluctantly mentioned leukemia. A bone marrow test confirmed the worst: acute myelomonocytic leukemia (Quill 1991).

The diagnosis devastated Diane. Raised in an alcoholic family, she had felt alone for much of her early life. She had had vaginal cancer as a young woman, and through much of her adult life had struggled with depression and her own alcoholism. Gradually, painfully, she had overcome these problems and had developed a strong sense of independence and confidence. Recently, her efforts had been paying off. She was abstinent from alcohol, and she had established strong relationships with her husband and son, several friends, and her physician.

The possibilities of technological intervention for this type of cancer offered cures 25 percent of the time, and the course of therapy would include such intrusive measures as induction chemotherapy, consolidation chemotherapy, and finally a bone marrow transplant. Each step along the way would mean hospitalization, severe side effects, and substantial risk of death.

Diane knew that she did not want to undergo chemotherapy and decided to live whatever time she had left outside the hospital. Her physician met with her and her family several times to discuss her options, risks of treatment, and the consequences of no treatment. She was adamant in her decision to seek only comfort care. The physician referred her to hospice care and tried to anticipate how to keep her comfortable in the time she had left.

It was important to Diane to maintain control of herself and her dignity during her dying. When this was no longer possible, she told her doctor, she wanted to die. It became clear to him that her fear of a lingering death would interfere with the quality of her time left. After discussing her feelings and desires with her family, Diane met with her doctor to discuss her "insomnia." It seemed to her physician that the security of having enough barbiturates available to commit suicide when and if the time came would leave her secure enough to live fully and concentrate on her present. She was not despondent and in fact was making deep, personal connections with family and friends. The doctor wrote a prescription with some misgivings but also with a feeling that he was setting her free to maintain dignity and control on her own terms until her death.

After several months, bone pain, weakness, fatigue, and

fevers began to dominate Diane's life. Although the physician, hospice workers, and family members tried to minimize her suffering and promote comfort, it was clear that the end was approaching. Diane faced increasing discomfort, dependence, and hard choices between pain and sedation. After saying good-bye to her friends and family, Diane deliberately overdosed on her barbiturate medication. The physician informed the medical examiner that she had died of acute leukemia.

## Martha

Martha is a 79-year-old Hispanic American from a large southwestern city with a sizable Hispanic population. She is married to Joe and the mother of one son, who lives in another state. Martha has always viewed herself as a spiritual person, interested in the varieties of the religious life. She attends a small Protestant church, the same one she and Joe have attended since they met at a party 30 years ago.

Martha has a history of hypertension, and she recently quit smoking. She was brought into the emergency room of a hospital near her home after suffering a massive stroke while reading the paper. The stroke left her in a coma. She was unresponsive to pain and showed no purposeful movement. Initially intubated as a precaution, Martha was successfully weaned from the respirator. Sustained by a nasogastric feeding tube, her treatment continued for all complications: infections were treated with antibiotics and gastrointestinal bleeding with blood transfusions. Martha's occasional respiratory distress was not serious enough for her to be reintubated. After two weeks, the consulting neurologist diagnosed Martha's condition as probably pervasive, permanent, and irreversible, commonly called a persistent vegetative state

(PVS), pending a confirming examination one week later. The subsequent neurological exam confirmed PVS, and she was transferred from the coronary care unit to another floor, while the hospital social worker sought placement for her in a nursing home or extended care facility.

When the family asked that all treatment be stopped and Martha be allowed to die, her nurse suggested an ethics consultation that included Joe, the couple's minister, Martha's attending physician, her nurse, and a representative from the hospital's ethics committee. The physician believed that Martha's condition was permanent and that she could live for twenty years with careful management. Joe stated that the quality of his wife's life was so diminished that he didn't think that she would want to live under these conditions, and again he asked that all treatment, including the feeding tube, be stopped. Disturbed by the direction of the conversation and by Joe's request, the family pastor claimed that each human life is a divine gift and that God teaches through life's accidents and contingencies.

After a lengthy discussion, and in light of Martha's condition, her surrogate's statements about her preferences, the legal precedent of a patient's right to refuse medical treatment, and the argument that her condition is irreversible, the physician agreed to discontinue nutrition and hydration as medical treatment. The minister left, quite upset, declaring that "starvation is starvation." The physician removed the feeding tube the following day, and Martha's care plan shifted to "comfort care only."

Two days later, Joe asked the physician to "do something" to hasten Martha's death. He could see no point in "stretching things out." The physician replied that such an act was beyond his professional responsibilities. Joe again asked him to do something, saying, "I'd do it myself, but I don't know how."

# CHAPTER TWO

# SOME QUESTIONS AND ANSWERS FOR STATE LEGISLATORS AND PUBLIC POLICY MAKERS

□ ■ □

Public policy makers ask a variety of questions relating to physician-assisted suicide and its many attendant issues. These questions often concern the underlying causes of current debate; the meaning of frequently used terms associated with PAS; and societal, legal, and religious attitudes and responses. We address some of these questions and concerns here while offering an overview of these issues—paying particular attention to religious concerns. We will also provide some conceptual resources for thinking about them.

**Is there a difference between euthanasia, terminating treatment, active euthanasia, passive euthanasia, and assisted suicide?**

People often use the general term *euthanasia* when they're actually referring to something quite different, and the confusion obscures important issues.

The word *euthanasia* is a combination of two Greek words that together mean "an easy death." The term has come to mean the direct taking of a terminally ill or dying person's life by another person, for compassionate reasons, but there are different ways in which the term can be used. Voluntary euthanasia is a form of suicide; it is taking one's life, with the assistance or intervention of another person. The first instance of voluntary euthanasia is popularly called *assisted suicide*. The Janet Adkins-Kevorkian case is such an instance.

When intentionally ending life to relieve suffering is achieved by another person's act (injecting the patient with potassium chloride, for example), that is called *active euthanasia*. When accomplished with the patient's consent (and usually at his or her request), the act is called *active, voluntary euthanasia*. Such active, voluntary euthanasia often occurs when a patient is too weak or otherwise unable to bring about his or her death and requests someone else (a physician, family member, or friend) to do so. The lethal injection Jack Kevorkian administered to Thomas Youk, aired by *60 Minutes* in November 1998, is an instance of active, voluntary euthanasia. Kevorkian did not simply provide the means for someone's suicide; he administered the lethal dose himself.

Euthanasia can also occur against the will of the patient. This is *involuntary euthanasia*. In addition, euthanasia sometimes happens without the patient's knowledge or consent but not necessarily against her will; this is called *nonvoluntary euthanasia*. Most people would consider these two forms of euthanasia immoral. A family member of a person with Alzheimer's, for example, might end the life of that person out of compassion, without having obtained the person's consent. Or, as in the case of Martha and her husband Joe, the spouse of someone in a persistent vegetative state could decide to take active measures to end that person's life, with no prior indication of the person's preference. This discussion will concentrate on issues surrounding a narrower definition of voluntary euthanasia as the taking of one's own life, albeit with the assistance of a physician, in other words, physician-assisted suicide.

## Is there a distinction between withholding or withdrawing life-sustaining treatment and instigating physician-assisted suicide? What is terminal sedation? How is that different from PAS?

There is much debate about the distinction between withholding or withdrawing life-sustaining treatment and instigating physician-assisted suicide. Many argue that there is no real difference, given that the predictable outcome—an earlier death—is the same. Others, including the U.S. Supreme Court, stress a clear distinction between the two: assisted suicide involves "active" assistance by a third party who acts with the patient to bring about the patient's death; withholding or withdrawing treatment, on the other hand, involves the parties standing by and awaiting a "passive death" (see Forum for State Health Policy Leadership and Center to Improve Care of the Dying 1998:37).

Suppose that Steve, the person with AIDS in the first case, had been placed on a respirator and also had a feeding tube inserted into his stomach. His condition is such that without these measures he would die. Even with such help, his condition would continue to deteriorate, but more slowly. Steve eventually insists that the respirator and the feeding tube—both forms of "life-sustaining," or "life-prolonging," treatment—be removed and that when he experiences cardiac or respiratory arrest, he not be resuscitated. Would stopping these measures and not resuscitating be considered euthanasia? Not in this case.

Stopping and withdrawing treatment here would be an acknowledgment that further treatment would do the patient little or no good. It would not restore him to good health and would only prolong the dying process. Furthermore, the burdens of the treatment (physical, psychological, social, and economic) and possibly the diminished quality of his life (pain and suffering, severe physical or mental impairments) could outweigh the treatment's long-run benefits. While most religious traditions recognize a responsibility to preserve life, they also recognize limits to that responsibility.

This notion is usually referred to as the principle of "burden/benefit" or "proportionate/disproportionate means." Generally, for a medical treatment to be morally obligatory, the benefits must outweigh the burdens. Until fairly recently, people called this the principle of "ordinary/extraordinary means."

The decision, then, to not initiate or to stop treatment is really a decision to stop doing what no longer benefits the patient or what has become unreasonably burdensome in order to let nature run its course. The intention is to stop interfering with the dying process, perhaps sooner than if the patient had received maximal treatment. In its 1990 ruling in *Cruzan v. Missouri Department of Health*, the U. S. Supreme Court recognized that individuals with decision-making capacity have a right to forgo any treatment, including life-sustaining treatment (ventilators, cardiopulmonary resuscitation, and the artificial provision of nutrition and hydration). These decisions—whether they are about initiating or discontinuing treatment—are referred to as *termination of treatment, withholding or withdrawing life-sustaining treatment, refusal of life-extending treatment,* and *allowing to die* or *letting die.*

## What are the legal issues surrounding physician-assisted suicide? What has the Supreme Court ruled, and what are the implications of its ruling?

Recent cases in the Ninth and Second Circuit Courts challenged state laws that banned assisted suicide in Washington and New York. The two courts held, on separate grounds, that these laws were unconstitutional to the extent that they banned physician-assisted suicide for terminally ill, mentally competent patients.

In the Ninth Circuit case (*Washington et al. v. Glucksberg*), a group of doctors and a not-for-profit organization that counsels terminally ill patients challenged Washington State's statute prohibiting physician-assisted suicide. The plaintiffs claimed that the law was unconstitutional because it violated the Due Process Clause of the Fourteenth Amendment to the U.S. Constitution. According to this argument, since no state shall make laws depriving an individual of essential liberties, a fundamental liberty protected under the Constitution is the right to choose the time and manner of one's own death. The U. S. Ninth District Circuit Court of Appeals agreed.

The question presented was whether Washington's prohibition against causing or aiding a suicide violates the Due Process Clause and whether the "liberty" especially protected by that clause includes a right to commit suicide, which itself includes a right to assistance in doing so. A description of the asserted fundamental right, or "liberty interest," at stake in this matter includes

1) The right to "determine the time and manner of one's death"
2) "The right to die"
3) "A liberty to choose how one dies"
4) "Control of one's final days"
5) "The right to choose a humane, dignified death"
6) "The liberty to shape death"

The Court analyzed the alleged "right" to assistance in committing suicide and noted that the due process clause protects fundamental rights that are deeply rooted in the nation's history and tradition. The history of the law's treatment of assisted suicide in this country has been and continues to be a rejection of nearly all efforts to permit it. Nowhere was a distinction made between individuals who are near death and those who are not. That being the case, the Court concluded that the alleged "right" to assistance in committing suicide is not a fundamental liberty protected by the due process clause. Moreover, the Court found that the state has a legitimate interest in the preservation of life and the ethics of the medical profession. Second, the Court noted that preventing suicide by offering palliative medicine and counseling shows significant success, and legalized physician-assisted suicide could make it more difficult for the state to protect depressed or mentally ill persons or those who are suffering from untreated pains or from suicidal impulses. Finally, permitting assisted suicide could lead to voluntary and perhaps involuntary euthanasia. In holding that Washington's ban on assisted suicide did not violate the Due Process Clause, the Court concluded that the ban involved legitimate government interests. Those interests include

1) "Prohibiting intentional killing" and "preserving human life"
2) Protecting "the young, elderly, and those suffering from untreated pain or from depression or other mental disorders"
3) Protecting the medical profession's integrity and ethics, and maintaining physicians' roles as healers
4) Protecting the poor, disabled, terminally ill, and persons in other vulnerable groups from indifference, prejudice, and psychological and financial pressure to end their lives

Further, the Court stated that, "[t]hroughout the Nation, Americans are engaged in an earnest and profound debate about the morality, legality, and practicality of physician-assisted suicide. Our holding permits this debate to continue, as it should in a democratic society."

In the Second Circuit case (*Vacco v. Quill*), three gravely ill persons challenged New York's statute banning assisted suicide on the grounds that the New York law violates the Fourteenth Amendment's Equal Protection Clause, which prohibits states from denying a person or class of persons within its jurisdiction the equal protection of the laws. In other words, "equal protection" requires that persons under like circumstances be given equal protection in the enjoyment of personal rights and the prevention and redress of wrongs. Plaintiffs claimed that the New York law permitting terminally ill, mentally competent persons to hasten their deaths by withdrawing life support systems treats differently terminally ill, mentally competent persons who want a physician to assist them in hastening their death. In other words, the New York statute prohibiting assisted suicide unfairly discriminates against terminally ill people who are not on life support. The Second Circuit agreed and found that withdrawing life-sustaining medical treatment was nothing more nor less than assisted suicide.

In reviewing *Vacco v. Quill*, the Supreme Court in 1997 disagreed with this judgment. It argued that the distinction between *letting* a patient die and *making* that patient die is important, logical, and well established. The Court further disagreed that such a distinction is "arbitrary" and "irrational." The line between the two acts may not always be clear, but it need not be. "Logic and contemporary practice support New York's judgment that the two acts are different, and New York may therefore, consistent with the Constitution, treat them differently."

Distinguishing between withdrawal and refusal of medical treatment and physician-assisted suicide, where both result in "hastening death," the Court looked to the fundamental legal principles of causation and intent. In the first principle—*causation*—a patient who refuses life-sustaining medical treatment dies from the underlying pathology, whereas a patient who ingests lethal medication prescribed by a physician dies from the medication. Under the principle of *intent*, a physician who honors a patient's wish to withdraw or withhold treatment intends to respect the patient's wishes. Similarly, aggressive palliative care intends to ease pain. The patient and physician need not necessarily intend death. A doctor who assists a suicide, however, must necessarily intend "that the patient be made dead." A patient committing suicide with a physician's assistance has the specific intent to die.

The Court notes these valid and important public interests, which easily satisfy the constitutional requirement that a legal classification bear a rational relation to some legitimate end. These ends may include

1) Prohibiting intentional killing
2) Preserving life
3) Preventing suicide
4) Maintaining the physician's role as the patient's healer
5) Protecting vulnerable people from indifference, prejudice, and psychological and financial pressure to end their lives
6) Avoiding a possible slide toward euthanasia

The Supreme Court ruling upholds these two state laws banning assisted suicide. However, it allows state legislators to permit and regulate physician-assisted suicide. In effect, the Supreme Court found that while there is no constitutional right to physician assisted suicide, states are free to permit it.

In response to the possibility that some states will legislate PAS, President Clinton signed the Federal Assisted Suicide Funding Restriction Act of 1997, which prohibits use of federal funds to support physician-assisted suicide.

**Talk about PAS continues in the media, grassroots movements in several states are seeking to legalize PAS, and medical publications continue to discuss it. Why has PAS become such a topic of ordinary conversation? Why now?**

Most people in our society have experienced something of medical technology's great successes. Today as never before, physicians are able to prolong life and cure disease, sometimes in very dramatic ways. But there's a reverse side. Physicians often use medical technology inappropriately and at a high price. People can become victims of technology: their dying can be prolonged beyond what is reasonable, and their lives can be extended at an extremely low quality. Medical technology can burden people with machines, procedures, tubes, and medications rather than enhance a state of well-being.

People today may be undergoing a loss of faith in the medical utopias promised a generation ago. Early transplant surgeons were cultural heroes. New discoveries and instruments were expected to enhance life in every way. Now medical technology is being given a second look. Many people seem worried that the way in which medical technology can be applied may prolong their dying in ways they do not want.

**Is medicine's success at prolonging dying the only fear that is at issue here?**

No. Medicine's *limits* also fuel the interest in assisted suicide. Medicine cannot cure all diseases nor suppress or alleviate all symptoms. People fear mental deterioration, the wasting away of their bodies, the embarrassment of disfigurement, and the loss of energy, control, and the ability to do things for themselves. They fear physical pain and many forms of psychological anguish. The cases that opened this discussion reflect many of these fears. For some people, assisted suicide may be a way to settle them.

People today are living longer. With longer life comes the possibility of more years of physical and mental decline. For some, chronic illness adds to the burden. The specter of nursing homes lingers on the horizon. Medicine, for all its discoveries, has not halted the aging process. For these reasons and others, physician-assisted suicide is seen as a palliative.

### Are there other driving forces in the debate?

A number of other concerns and attitudes play a role in the debate. For example, both health care professionals and the general public recognize the inadequacy of pain relief and pain management near the end of life (Solomon et al. 1993; The SUPPORT Principal Investigators 1995). While the debate over PAS has focused attention on improving palliative or comfort care measures, there is still a widespread fear of uncontrolled pain at the end of life.

A second force driving an interest in PAS is the cost of health care. The past decade of literature on medical costs at the end of life does not support the hypothesis that the rise in costs is due largely to the use of high-tech medical care by the dying. Nonetheless, a disproportionate amount of healthcare money is spent in the last six months of life (Scitovsky 1991). More than two-thirds of all families confronted with the prolonged illness and death of a loved one suffer the additional indignity of economic hardship and even poverty (Covinsky et al. 1996). Assisted suicide may seem one way to lower healthcare costs and relieve families of the financial burden of end-of-life care.

More philosophically, a contributing factor is the contemporary American emphasis on "freedom of choice," or autonomy. Some regard physician-assisted suicide as the "ultimate choice," in that it offers people control over their own death. It gives the patient a say in when and how she is going to die, providing a sense of control over the dying process. The concept of control is central to the debate: Who is going to control when and how I die? Who controls my destiny near the point of death? Much of the fear surrounding death has to do with precisely this: Do I lose control?

The rancorous debates about PAS usually ignore complex philosophical and theological questions. Do we really want complete control over our lives? Do our lives belong to us to do with as we wish? Are there limits to our freedom to choose for ourselves? Does autonomy extend to actively ending one's life? Does so much emphasis on the rights of the individual give short shrift to our interconnectedness? Does it minimize responsibilities to family members, to the communities in which we live, and to society as a whole? At base, these are questions about *meaning*—the meaning of rights, autonomy, and relatedness to others and to the Other.

Other issues also pose challenges in the PAS debate, whether we are religious or not. What does life *mean* for a human being? Is human life merely biological? Or is it something else, essentially? This raises the question of *personhood*. What does it mean to be a person? Can one cease to be a person while still in some sense remaining *alive*? What do we mean by *quality of life*? At what point, if any, is human life no longer worth continuing?

How are we to understand human finitude, that is, the fact that our lives and abilities are limited? What meaning do we give to dependency, to decline and aging, to pain and suffering, to illness and death, to human existence as a whole? Some people say we are experiencing a crisis about the meaning of life and that, ironically, physician-assisted suicide appears to offer an effective remedy for dealing with some of life's negatives. The way in which we answer the above questions, both individually and as a society, will affect how we evaluate the PAS debate.

### What about religion? Is it partly responsible for increased interest in PAS?

Probably. Some would argue that a weakening in fundamental religious beliefs about the existence of God or an afterlife supports physician-assisted suicide. If there is no God, then one's life is not a gift of the Creator but entirely one's own. If we are not responsible to an ultimate Other, then our individual autonomy increases. Religiously based injunctions against the taking of innocent human life lose their force. Finally, some would say, if there is no afterlife, we need not worry about ultimate accountability for PAS.

### Do religious believers sometimes support PAS?

Yes. We're seeing changes in certain religious and moral beliefs, not wholesale rejection of them. Some people acknowledge that human life is a gift and that we humans are caretakers. Under certain circumstances, ending human life is not outside the scope of responsible stewardship. Some religious people view physician-assisted suicide as a form of such stewardship and a legitimate exercise of human intelligence and choice.

Many Christians, for example, feel that because we

humans are self-determining agents created in the image of God, we have a right and a responsibility to choose whether to end our lives by means of assisted suicide. When we can no longer serve God or others by remaining alive, it is not wrong to exercise our freedom of choice to bring about our own death—or ask others to help us.

Others maintain that PAS should not be lumped with other forms of prohibited killing. The motive for the killing and the circumstances surrounding it are different. The moral evil present in other forms of taking innocent life may not be present. Hastening a person's dying at their request is not morally equal to taking a person's life against their will.

Still other religious people see assisted suicide as an appropriate moral response to pain and suffering. Some argue that we violate our inherent dignity when the overuse of medical technology forces us to endure pain and suffering. God's purposes are to relieve our suffering, they believe, and PAS provides a compassionate way of ending unredemptive suffering.

With some religious believers increasingly receptive to PAS, the challenge facing religious communities in the months and years ahead will be to confront these and other new directions head-on and to assess them honestly and critically.

### I typically hear that religious people are against assisted suicide because of a belief in the sanctity of human life. What are other religious arguments opposing physician-assisted suicide?

There are a variety of religiously based arguments against suicide and assisted suicide, and the sanctity of life as a gift from God is certainly one shared by several of the major religious traditions. Certain traditions within Judaism, Christianity, and Islam, for example, believe that we are not our own but hold our lives in trust for God. According to this tenet, God has created each person for a purpose, and we are each accountable to God for how we live and how we die. We violate God's sovereignty and interrupt God's purposes when we deliberately end our lives or the lives of others. Also, if we believe that God created us to live in community, caring for others and working to achieve a common good, self-killing could be seen necessarily to diminish our interpersonal bonds. By introducing socially sanctioned killing of the innocent, PAS risks eliminating those most in need of human fellowship from society.

Second, some religious people argue that pain and suffering are inevitable consequences of our finite human condition. We should strive to eliminate pain and suffering by morally acceptable means, such as appropriate palliative care measures, not by PAS.

Third, that a choice for death exists does not make that choice right. God asks people to use their freedom of choice in accord with their religious values. Acts that deliberately end innocent human lives, even at their request, deny God's purposes. What's more, legalized assisted suicide jeopardizes one's choice to remain alive. One can imagine a world in which a person would have to account to others for a decision to continue living. Life as such would no longer be a given; it would require justification.

### Have religious communities staked out positions on this issue?

Most religious groups have long traditions regarding death and dying and the taking of human life. They also have long-standing beliefs about the sacredness of life, the nature of human beings, suffering, salvation, the existence of an afterlife, the existence of a deity, and the deity's relation to humankind. These and other basic beliefs can inform thinking about physician-assisted suicide; many religious traditions have issued statements opposing physician-assisted suicide.

A word of caution, however. Not all members of a particular group hold a uniform position on PAS. Some people who believe in the sacredness of life are rethinking their position on PAS. It could be, moreover, that in the years ahead some groups may modify their official stance on the issue.

### How widespread is the support for PAS? Is what we're seeing a media effect, or is there, in fact, growing sentiment for legalization?

Surveys of the general public appear to show substantial support at least for the idea of physician-assisted suicide. That support has been generally consistent over time. In 1990, 72 percent of Americans felt that doctors should be able to help end the lives of the hopelessly ill at the request of the patient (Gest 1990). In a 1998 poll, that figure was 74 percent ("Americans say...", p. 53).

The numbers in a 1996 *Washington Post* poll tell another side of the story. In this telephone survey, 51 percent of the people polled thought assisted suicide should be legalized. However, 55 percent of those who thought so were white, as opposed to 20 percent of those who were African American. While 58 percent of those with incomes over $75,000 said the practice should be legal, only 37 percent of those with incomes under $15,000 did. Men and women responded differently: 54 percent of the men felt PAS should be legalized, but only 47 percent of the women agreed. There were similar breakdowns by age: 52 percent of those between 18 and 29 years of age thought PAS should be legalized; 35 percent of those over 70 agreed. In short, those who feel relatively powerful in our society are far more comfortable with the notion of physician-assisted suicide than are more vulnerable groups (Rosenbaum 1996).

Polls are tricky. Their accuracy depends on the questions the pollsters ask, how they ask, the circumstances in which they ask, who is asked, and how the respondents understand the questions. Nevertheless, the results still may be telling.

### Isn't PAS legal in Holland? If it's not a big problem there, why should it be here?

Both euthanasia and physician-assisted suicide are more widely practiced, or at least more widely acknowledged, in Holland than in the U.S., yet there is a fair amount of misunderstanding about these phenomena. First, under the current Dutch penal code, euthanasia and assisted suicide, while not legal practices, have been decriminalized. In practice, the state will not prosecute physicians who perform euthanasia or assisted suicide if the cases are exceptional and the physicians follow strict criteria.

In Holland, the request for euthanasia or assisted suicide must be entirely voluntary, free of all external coercion, and must originate from the patient (this presupposes that the patient's request is well considered and persistent). Furthermore, the patient's suffering must be intolerable and without prospect of improvement (so, in a sense, assisted suicide is a last resort, other alternatives having been considered and found wanting). Finally, the physician who performs euthanasia or assisted suicide must first consult with an experienced physician colleague.

Either the coroner or physician must report to the police that an incident has occurred. The police in turn report to the district attorney, who then decides whether or not to prosecute. In all the prosecuted cases between 1973 and 1983, the first two conditions above were deemed essential by judges who reached verdicts of not guilty, acquittal, or conditional punishments. They were also the conditions that permitted district attorneys to dismiss such cases. Some courts and judges mentioned the third criterion as important. Since 1984, all courts have employed the three criteria, which have become the necessary conditions for the acceptable or tolerable (though not legal) practice of physician-assisted suicide.

In summary, it would be far more accurate to say that a certain professional and public tolerance exists in Holland with regard to assisted suicide, though the practice remains illegal. The Dutch generally recognize that ethically and legally there is much to debate.

### In practice, what has been the Dutch experience with PAS? Have there been abuses of the system?

The lack of hard data makes it difficult to tell whether there have been abuses of the criteria. One estimate suggests that there are between 2,000 and 10,000 cases of euthanasia and physician-assisted suicide per year out of a population of 15 million (Van der Maas et al. 1992:193-94). According to the Remmelink Report, a study of the practice of physician-assisted suicide and euthanasia, in 1990 there were some 2,300 cases of euthanasia at the patient's request, 400 cases of assisted suicide, and about 1,000 cases in which physicians terminated patients' lives without their consent. Fourteen percent of the patients who were killed without consent were fully competent (Van der Maas, *supra* note 60, at 61). Of the 130,000 deaths reported in the Netherlands in 1990, in addition to the 1,000 explicitly identified cases of active involuntary euthanasia, there were 4,941 cases in which physicians reported that they gave morphine not simply to relieve pain but for the purpose of terminating life—without a fully competent patient's knowledge. In other words, almost 5,000 Dutch patients in 1990 had their lives intentionally ended by a physician who did not obtain their consent. 27 percent of these non-consenting patients were fully competent.

Physicians also flout the rules governing voluntary euthanasia. In the 2,300 cases of voluntary euthanasia, 19 percent of physicians did not consult another physician, 54 percent failed to record the proceedings in writing, and 72 percent concealed the fact that patients died by voluntary euthanasia (Fenigson 1991:339ff; May 1996:38-39). Opponents of physician-assisted suicide argue that these figures indicate that the Netherlands has begun to move down the slippery slope from a judicial sanctioning of PAS motivated by the right to individual self-determination and the compassionate alleviation of suffering to unchecked, non-consensual termination of human life (Canady 1998).

### People who oppose or are unsure about PAS often talk about the "slippery slope." What's that about?

"Slippery slope" is simply a way of saying that once a person or society starts down a certain path, gravity will pull them farther along it. Applied to physician-assisted suicide, it means that if we allow physicians to end the lives of the immediately dying at their request, it won't stop there. The argument goes like this: Suppose legislatures legalize physician-assisted suicide. Wouldn't it also be logical to legalize PAS for those who are terminally ill but not yet dying (for example, individuals with Huntington's disease, multiple sclerosis, or Lou Gehrig's disease, or even those in the early stages of cancer, Alzheimer's, or AIDS)? What about people who are incurable but non-terminal (people left severely impaired after an accident, dialysis patients, diabetics, quadriplegics, stroke victims, or people in a persistent vegetative state)? If it makes sense to relieve a short period of suffering for the dying patient, wouldn't it make more sense to relieve a longer span of suffering for the non-dying but terminal or incurable patient? Why limit the exercise of autonomy to people who appear closer to dying?

**So we expand PAS to the non-terminal and the incurable. Is this where the line gets drawn?**
What about those who are no longer able to make decisions for themselves but have not made provisions in advance? Take the case of Martha. Shouldn't she also have the opportunity to have her pain and suffering relieved? Under the doctrine of "substituted judgment," one might argue—as her husband does—that Martha would not want to live this poor quality of life and would want assistance in ending her life were she now able to choose. There is a shift here from voluntary to nonvoluntary euthanasia, but why not? Why should we deprive those who are incompetent of relief?

And if substituted judgment can serve as a legitimizing basis for physician-assisted death, why not also "best interests"? If a person leaves no substantial indication of what he or she would have chosen, might not decision-makers argue that it is in that individual's "best interests" to have his or her life ended? And if this logic applies to adults, why not also to handicapped newborns and terminally ill children? Why not to the mentally ill?

In other words, what some fear is that assisted suicide might lead, logically and in practice, down the slope to include more categories of individuals, even to the point of legitimizing nonvoluntary euthanasia. Of course, the most serious scenario would be to allow for the practice of involuntary euthanasia, that is, ending a person's life explicitly against their will.

These possibilities concerned the Supreme Court in its deliberations over the Ninth and Second Circuit cases.

### Don't people have a right to die?

The phrase "right to die" is actually quite ambiguous, and it could mean several things. It could refer to the "right to refuse treatment" or the "right to be allowed to die," that is, the right not to have one's dying interfered with, the right to be free from the imposition of unwanted medical procedures. Taken this way, there is generally little disagreement about this right when it is recognized morally and legally.

But the "right to die" could also mean the "right to kill oneself," to commit suicide without the interference of others. To date, such a claim has no legal recognition. Many people would still argue that suicide is a moral right flowing from our right to self-determination and autonomy.

### Speaking of autonomy, isn't assisted suicide ultimately an individual matter, a matter of personal choice, a decision among patient, physician, and family? Why get sidetracked with all these moral, religious, and legal debates?

True, assisted suicide is a matter of personal choice, to some extent. But it's not quite that simple. Many philosophers, theologians, and social scientists believe that people are not merely isolated, self-determining individuals. They are social by nature and connect to others in many different ways. Because of that interconnectedness and the impact of individual acts of suicide upon others, PAS is also a social issue and, therefore, a matter of public policy. It is unrealistic to think that individuals go about choosing to die without the choice having some impact upon family members and friends, the physicians they ask to assist, the communities of which they are a part, and even society as a whole. These entities can be, are, and will be affected by instances of assisted suicide. In addition, individuals' actions reflect and give expression to values and beliefs, which are formed in some part by the society around them. The more people perform a certain action and the more frequently they perform it, the more those values and beliefs get expressed. The effect is cumulative and eventually influences the moral tone or character of a society. Thus, individual acts of assisted suicide have consequences and implications beyond the individual decision-makers. As a result, policy makers need to be concerned not only with individual welfare but also with social welfare. Many people struggle with these tensions. They believe that certain cases justify assisted suicide but are concerned by the possible social consequences of a public policy allowing physician-assisted suicide.

Taking human life, whether justified or not, is always a matter of moral concern. Though difficult, we gain much from public moral argument. For believers, religious questions are central to this argument.

**You mention legislation. Are there pressures to legislate PAS?**

Yes, there are pressures both to legalize and to criminalize PAS, and they are likely to increase. For example, efforts to legalize PAS in states like California, Washington, and Florida have failed; efforts in Oregon have succeeded. Representatives and senators who haven't addressed these kinds of moral questions are under great pressure, often from interest groups, to do so. Already state legislators involved with the issue have been at work in their states. For a list of states considering assisted suicide legislation, see Appendix A.

Meanwhile, the public has responded, pro and con, to the actions of Jack Kevorkian. The media propels the issue to people's attention and generates a sense of urgency. This sort of pressure can translate into a push to legislate.

**What are the main arguments for and against legalizing PAS?**

On a concrete level, proponents of physician-assisted suicide argue that it already takes place. Legalization would regulate the practice and ensure safeguards against abuses.

Philosophical and legal arguments for legalization claim that just as a person has the right to determine the course of his or her own life, a person also has the right to determine the course of his or her own dying. Based on claims of personal autonomy, this point of view argues that if a terminally ill person seeks assistance from a physician, the physician ought to provide it, as long as the person makes his or her request freely and rationally.

There are two objections to this argument. First, some argue that true autonomy is rarely possible, or never possible, since most choices are socially formed. In addition, terminal illness can cause depression and other psychiatric disturbances, which can affect "autonomy" and "rationality." Second, a person should not be obligated to do what is morally wrong at another's request, even if that request is made freely and rationally. Since suicide is wrong, the argument goes, the physician has no obligation to assist in it.

Countering these two objections are those who argue that eans to bring about that death.

Opponents of PAS argue that it is possible to treat virtually all pain and relieve virtually all suffering. Such arguments affirm the dying process as a positive, transformative experience of new intimacy and spiritual growth for patient, family, and caregivers. Where physicians cannot control pain, the argument goes, complete sedation is preferable to suicide.

The counter-argument: assisted suicide is merciful in cases where physicians cannot treat pain or suffering. Suffering cannot guarantee a positive, transformative experience. Furthermore, because complete sedation means that the patient can no longer communicate or perceive others, it can be considered equivalent to death. Why not allow more direct methods of bringing about death?

Probably the most basic argument opposing physician-assisted suicide advanced by philosophers and theologians is the intrinsic wrongness of killing. The taking of human life is simply wrong, as stated by the biblical commandment, "Thou shall not kill."

A second argument against PAS states that permitting physicians to assist in suicide, even in sympathetic cases, will lead to situations of involuntary euthanasia in which patients are killed against their will (the slippery-slope argument). Therefore, society should not permit the practice, even if assisted death is one's personal choice and individual right.

Cost pressures, greed, laziness, insensitivity, and other factors affecting physicians can contribute to this abuse. Proponents argue that adequate safeguards can be devised to protect against these potential abuses.

A third argument against legalizing assisted suicide is that more vulnerable individuals—the disabled, the elderly, the poor—might feel a "duty to die" because of the excessive financial and emotional strain their illness places on family members and society at large. If society legalizes assisted suicide, opponents fear that a burden will be placed on people to justify their continued existence, particularly as society's commitment to disabled and dependent persons weakens. Proponents of PAS agree that supportive services to the chronically and terminally ill, such as palliative care, should be enhanced.

Also, though efforts to develop and deliver comprehensive palliative care services have improved, effective pain management and end-of-life comfort care can be difficult to obtain. Legalized assisted suicide might divert attention from these efforts and retard efforts to improve comfort care. If PAS is easily available, people might choose suicide over treatable misery without considering other available options such as pain management, counseling, and therapy (Merritt 1998: 39). Proponents point to Oregon, claiming with some justification that palliative care services have improved since the Death with Dignity Act was passed in 1994 ("State of Assisted Suicide in the U.S," p. 51).

Finally, opponents to PAS are concerned with the physician's role. Doctors should not kill; the Hippocratic Oath prohibits it. The physician must save lives, not take them. Permitting physicians to kill patients would undermine the public's trust in the medical profession. A counter view is that many people want physicians to act to relieve them of unbearable pain and suffering, preserving their dignity, even if that means assistance in dying.

### Is PAS legal in any states now?

Oregon is the only state that has legalized assisted suicide. A voter-approved ballot initiative passed in 1994, and an effort to repeal the Oregon Death with Dignity Act was defeated in 1997.

Assisted suicide is not legal in the other 49 states or in the District of Columbia. Thirty-six states outlaw assisted suicide under criminal codes, and nine under common law. In 1998, Kansas, Oklahoma, and Virginia adopted expansions of their assisted suicide-criminal laws, broadening the definition of assisting a suicide and authorizing a variety of penalties for any healthcare provider who assists in a suicide. According to *Choice in Dying*, a nonprofit organization, the four remaining states—North Carolina, Utah, Ohio, and Wyoming—are unclear about their positions. Among these four, North Carolina, Utah, and Wyoming do not have statutes prohibiting assisted suicide and have abolished their common law criminal language. A 1996 ruling by the Ohio Supreme Court found assisted suicide not to be a crime when very specific facts are presented as justification. It is unclear how that ruling will apply to future cases, however (Merritt 1998:40).

### Is there data from Oregon on the experiences of physicians and patients surrounding assisted suicide?

The Oregon Death with Dignity Act allows terminally ill state residents to receive from their physicians prescriptions for self-administered lethal medications. Information on 23 persons who received prescriptions for lethal medications in 1998 under the Act was reported to the Oregon Health Division. Of the 23, fifteen died after taking their lethal medication, six died from their underlying illnesses, and two were still alive as of January 1, 1999. These 15 people accounted for five of every 10,000 deaths in Oregon in 1998. The median age of the 15 patients was 69 years; eight were male; and all 15 were white. Thirteen of the 15 had cancer. PAS was not disproportionately chosen by terminally ill Oregonians who were poor, uneducated, uninsured, fearful of impoverishment, lacking end-of-life care, or concerned about being a burden to their families. Only one expressed concern about inadequate pain control.

During the first year of legalized physician-assisted suicide in Oregon, the decision to request and use a prescription for lethal medication was associated with concern about loss of autonomy or control of bodily functions, not with fear of intractable pain or concern about financial loss. The researchers found that the choice of PAS was not associated with level of education or health insurance coverage.

Fourteen physicians wrote prescriptions for lethal medications. For some of them, participating in physician-assisted suicide exacted an emotional toll. Physicians reported that their participation led to feelings of isolation: they felt unable to share their experiences with others because they feared ostracism by patients and colleagues. Forty percent of the patients who received prescriptions were unable to initiate the process with the first physician they approached and had to request a prescription from a second or third doctor. It is possible that fears about public perception and disapproval influence the willingness of physicians to participate in PAS under the Oregon Death with Dignity Act (Chin et al. 1999).

### What's so bad about legislation? Why shouldn't we have a public policy that legalizes physician-assisted suicide?

Given the course of events over the last decade, including the recent Supreme Court decision, the point of legislation is upon us. In discussions over physician-assisted suicide, the issue of morality in the individual case frequently is conflated with the issue of the morality of a public policy that legalizes the practice. Many would argue that these are distinct but related issues: the first is a matter of individual morality, while the second is one of social morality. Many people might believe that one or more of the cases presented in chapter one justifies assisted suicide. Many others would say, however, that such cases do not support allowing assisted suicide on a societal scale. Conversely, a public policy permitting physician-assisted suicide does not necessarily settle the moral justifiability of such suicide in individual cases. Different considerations and criteria come into play when we move from an individual to a societal context and vice versa.

For example, have we adequately considered the meaning of autonomy? How does autonomy operate in a social context? Have we sufficiently thought through the probable and possible consequences, good and bad, of either allowing or disallowing this measure? Can the problems contributing to a desire for PAS be remedied by other means? Have all reasonable alternatives been tried? Could it be that legalized PAS would leave unresolved the root problems associated with care of the terminally ill and dying, and deal with only the symptoms? How would a policy of legalized assisted suicide be reconciled with basic moral convictions as well as with the beliefs of most religious traditions? Many such questions deserve careful consideration before we try to "settle" the issue through legislation.

## What issues need to be addressed in a legalizing statute?

If a state legislature is considering a statute to legalize physician-assisted suicide, legislators will need to consider a number of issues. Included in these are adequate safeguards to protect the public against abuses like the kind that regularly occur in Holland. The *Model State Act to Authorize and Regulate Physician-Assisted Suicide* was drafted by a number of experts and published in the *Harvard Journal on Legislation* (January 1997) and includes the commonly mentioned safeguards.

1) Terminal illness: The model statute follows the Medicare hospice benefit eligibility requirement in defining terminal illness as "a bodily disorder likely to cause the patient's death within six months." Because of the uncertainty and subjectivity surrounding medical prognosis, the language allows for some flexibility of "reasonable medical judgment." A lack of precision in the policy language concerns PAS opponents, as does the fact that physicians cannot pinpoint with certainty how much time a patient has remaining in his or her life. The data available for such predictions are available only for a few illnesses. Proponents might argue, therefore, that restrictions on assisted suicide should exclude an arbitrary prognosis of terminal illness. Since some benchmark would be necessary in defining terminal illness, PAS legislation might require more specificity. Some claim that the severity of an illness or the likelihood of recovery, rather than length of life, should be used as qualifiers.

2) Voluntary choice: The model court statute also requires that the patient's decision be voluntary and uncoerced. The fear that an ill person might be persuaded or forced into a request for assisted suicide is a major concern of any legislation, but a procedure to ensure independent, voluntary choice is somewhat arbitrary. Typically, those proposed procedures entail a two-week waiting period and multiple requests from the patient to ensure voluntariness. Two questions often arise: Would poverty, inadequate palliative care, or social pressures push vulnerable people into seeking assisted suicide? How is one to determine when such factors constitute a violation of free choice?

3) Suffering: The model act states that a patient seeking PAS must have a terminal illness or an "intractable and unbearable illness"—a "bodily disorder that cannot be cured or successfully palliated and that causes such severe suffering that a patient prefers death." The act does not define suffering, perhaps because it is such a subjective condition.

4) Decisional capacity: To protect people incapable of making healthcare decisions, informed consent procedures commonly used in healthcare decision-making are recommended in the model act. Physicians would follow these procedures when patients request assistance and at the time of suicide. Therefore, a physician must attest that the request "is not the result of a distortion of the patient's judgment due to clinical depression or any other mental illness." Other suggestions would preclude distortion of judgment due to medication. As for a definition of decisional

capacity, there is not complete agreement. Nor is there clarity on what to do about people who opt for assisted suicide now, for fear of declining capacity in the future.

5) Physician assistance: Because of the emphasis on diagnosis, prognosis, treatment options (including hospice care), and the demands of informed consent, there is almost universal agreement that, should assisted suicide be legalized, the practice must involve a physician. The model act typically requires that physicians provide a patient with the information necessary for informed choice and discuss the information with him or her. Additionally, physicians must document in the medical record discussions with patients. The desire for physician participation is understandable, given the general public's confidence in physicians' knowledge and expertise. However, even if society decides to legalize assisted suicide as a potential benefit to people that physicians can offer, solid data regarding levels of medications or other lethal alternatives to ensure effective and efficient suicides remains unavailable.

6) Witnessing and continuity requirements: Model legislation requires that two adults witness conversations between the patient and physician. In addition, the physician must obtain a written evaluation from a mental health practitioner that the patient is not depressed or mentally ill and is fully informed. Finally, such model statutes usually require two requests by the patient, with a waiting period of perhaps fourteen days between them.

7) Documentation and reporting: One protection against abuse involves documentation requirements that would include medical history, prognosis, current condition, reasons for the patient's request for assisted suicide, and a record of discussions with patient and family. Such documentation would have to include a clear expression of the patient's choice—not merely an "informed consent" to the procedure, but a documentation of the patient's active request, including what treatment alternatives were discussed with the patient and what palliatives were offered.

In addition, the performance of the assisted suicide would have to be reported to an appropriate external agency. Suggestions of such an agency include the coroner, the Centers for Disease Control, or Health and Human Services. Detailed information about cases of assisted suicide and the effectiveness of the process would be available for review (Battin 1994:177).

These safeguard proposals are controversial since none of them are ironclad. Proponents of PAS believe that they represent a reasonable effort to prevent abuses. Opponents argue that even one abuse is too many.

### So should we do nothing?

Doing nothing on the legislative front, some people say, would be better than doing something or trying to do too much prematurely. It is safe to say that a group of the most seasoned and respected ethicists and the most experienced medical, legal, and clergy personnel would counsel to "go slowly." Take time. Resist stampedes. Don't let interest groups pressure you into premature or sweeping decisions.

Doing nothing on the legislative front, of course, doesn't mean doing nothing at all. There are opportunities for public education, discussion, and debate. Religious communities, health care and educational institutions, health-related organizations, professional societies, and senior citizens' organizations can all make contributions. Keeping people informed and involved is one of the most important tasks for churches and synagogues, hospitals, and universities with a public concern.

Town meetings and open forums held across the country are examples of non-legislative attempts at furthering discussion. The more such meetings and forums occur, the more likely the public will equip itself to participate thoughtfully in addressing an issue in which it has so much at stake. Currently, many people don't know quite what position to take, what outcomes to pursue, what laws to write, or what beliefs to hold. Much can be gained by a period of listening and learning and by concerted efforts to address the treatment problems and issues that assisted suicide brings to the fore.

Furthermore, premature efforts to legislate could well polarize society in a manner similar to the abortion controversy. We can recognize that, in one sense, we're all on the same side on this issue—that we want to make dying as humane as possible. Perhaps more discussion, increased understanding, and honest and cooperative dialogue can help avoid some of the polarization.

Going slowly with PAS legislation does not preclude continuing to work to improve and expand end-of-life care, though some fear it will. There have been and continue to be advances in pain management and renewed attention to emotional and spiritual care at the end of life.

**It seems that the PAS issue affects just about everyone and that everyone has a stake in how it's resolved.**

The issue clearly affects doctors, nurses, and hospital administrators, in addition to patients and their families. Depending on how we read PAS, health care professionals might be asked to participate in humane care, a betrayal of their profession, or even a criminal act. They might respond with mercy to cries of pain or have to respond to homicide charges. Healthcare professionals cannot afford not to think about this issue. At stake is their responsibility to care for the terminally ill and dying as well as the very meaning of their profession.

### What do others have at stake?

Clergy clearly have much at stake. Not only do they help keep religious and moral traditions alive and relevant, they counsel families in times of agony and distress. If they stand in the way of loving acts in the name of laws claimed to be divine, they seem cruel. If they stand with patients who want their pain and suffering ended, they may be accused of betraying their deepest beliefs, violating the divine will, and eroding respect for human life.

The issue of assisted suicide also affects lawyers and lawmakers. Legislators who ignore this issue or oppose PAS legalization will be criticized as ignorant or inhumane. Those who support it will be accused of undermining societal respect for life, endorsing homicide, and the like.

The person on the street also has much at stake. Any of us may someday encounter a loved one pleading for relief of pain and suffering. More fundamentally, we all have to die and the many ways of prolonging a life today can make the end of life more dreadful than it used to be. When people talk about assisted suicide, they are in some sense talking about themselves.

## This personal angle does seem to make PAS a special case.

It may be important to talk about PAS in terms of specific cases, with real names and life stories. Each of us can *become* such a case, and all of us are living out such stories. That is why we read ourselves into others' narratives, whether positively ("I could see myself doing that") or negatively ("What a horrible thing for anyone to do; I wouldn't").

Some ethical issues in health care attract only elites and experts. *My* living and dying, *my* life story finds no one more concerned than I am. It's partly for this reason—along with an aging population—that the public is becoming more informed and involved in the PAS debate.

## With everyone having a stake in the matter, it makes sense that everyone's voice should be heard.

We need to pay particular attention to the experiences and insights of those people living through the kinds of pain and suffering that give rise to requests for physician-assisted suicide—those who are terminally ill, dying, or elderly with debilitating burdens. We should listen with great care to the family members and intimate friends who accompany these individuals through their ordeals. We should also listen to the physicians and nurses who see illness and suffering first-hand and try their best to remedy or alleviate that suffering within the limits of their own professional and personal belief systems and commitments. The insight and wisdom based on healthcare providers' experiences will be invaluable.

Others, too, have contributions to make from the perspective of their own life stories and professional engagements. Lawmakers call our attention to what is good for society as a whole. Their primary interest will be with developing a viable public policy. Clergy and religious leaders will likely attempt to keep the resources of their traditions in the forefront of the debate and draw out the implications and the wisdom of those traditions for the members of their communities.

All people bring to these issues their own fundamental beliefs, their own answers to life's basic questions. There is much at stake in the PAS debate about the way we value life—individual and communal lives. This commitment drives those who will actively participate—through interest groups or in a less organized way—in the debates surrounding PAS policy, as well as the less vocal majority who are also watching and listening. Clearly, those with religious beliefs and values aren't the only ones who take assisted suicide seriously, and there are many perspectives to consider. All the more reason to give assisted suicide a full airing before we determine policy.

CHAPTER | THREE

# VIEWS OF THE MAJOR
# FAITH TRADITIONS

☐ ☐ ■

The attitudes of various religious bodies toward physician-assisted suicide are central to any discussion of its morality and legalization. For this reason, we present summaries of the thinking of several major faith traditions. Physician-assisted suicide is our primary focus, but we also include, when available, denominational positions on forgoing life-sustaining treatment.

A brief treatment of the authoritative weight and binding force of its position on assisted suicide prefaces each presentation. Needless to say, this authority varies widely among the religious groups. The teachings of some traditions with regard to assisted suicide are prescriptive; of others, instructive. In some traditions, members are to obey, while in others, members are guided by their consciences. Many denominations do not have anything resembling an "official" position. Some have not given any specific attention to physician-assisted suicide, while others expect to take it up in the near future.

## Judaism

Although there are differences in the weight given to various sources of Jewish law, there appears to be a consensus among the Orthodox, Conservative, Reconstructionist, and Reform branches of Judaism that assisted suicide and euthanasia are not morally justified. This position is grounded in the Torah, the first five books of the Hebrew scriptures, which contain the earliest written traditions and laws of the people, and in rabbinical sources.

Judaism prohibits murder in all circumstances, and it views all forms of active euthanasia as the equivalent of murder (M. *Semahot* 1:1-2; M. *Shabbat* 23:5; and B. *Shabbat* 151b). That is true even if the patient asks for death. Because each person's body belongs to God, the patient does not have the right to commit suicide or to enlist the aid of others in the act; and anybody who aids in such a plan commits murder. No human being has the right to destroy or even damage God's property (Cf. Deuteronomy 20:19; B. *Bava Kamma* 8:6,7; S.A. *Hoshen Mishpat* 420:1, 31).

The Conservative Movement's Committee on Jewish Law and Standards has adopted a rabbinical ruling (teshuvah) by Rabbi Elliot Dorff affirming, among other issues, that

1) Suicide is a violation of Jewish law and of the sacred trust of our lives given us by God.

2) Assisting a suicide is also a violation of Jewish law and God's sacred trust of life. No human being may take his or her own life, ask others to help, or assist in such an effort.

3) Patients and their caregivers nevertheless have the tradition's permission to withhold or withdraw impediments to the natural process of dying.

4) Physicians must assure that patients are given sufficient pain medication as part of their duty to provide medical care, as mandated in Jewish law.

5) In the context of nuclear families, divorce, and far-flung families, the mitzvah of *biqqur holim* (visiting the sick) becomes all the more imperative in our day to counteract the loneliness that terminally ill patients often face. Individual Jews and synagogues should see this as an important priority of their Jewish commitments.

6) Requests for assistance in suicide are often an expression of the patient's extreme suffering, despair, psychiatric depression, and loneliness. The Jewish tradition bids us to express our compassion in ways that effectively respond to the patient's suffering while adhering to our mandate to respect the divine trust of life. Among such options is final care at home, with the help of palliative ministrations including hospice care, to provide the social and emotional support severely sick people need. The approach of death can provide an opportunity for the patient, family, and friends to have meaningful closure and final reconciliation. (Dorff 1991, 3-51).

The Jewish attitude toward euthanasia as well as toward suicide is based on the premise that "only He who gives life may take it away." For Judaism, human life is "created in the image of God." Although all life is God's creation and good, human life is related to God in a special way: it is sacred. The sanctity of human life prescribes that in any situation short of self-defense or martyrdom, human life should be treated as an end in itself. Thus, it may not be terminated or shortened out of considerations to the patient's convenience or usefulness—or even out of sympathy with the patient's suffering. Euthanasia, then, may not be performed in the interest of the patient or of anyone else. Individual autonomy is secondary to the sanctity of human life. In Judaism, suicide and euthanasia are both forms of prohibited homicide. No human life is any more or less sacred than any other (Feldman and Rosner 1984, p. 106).

## Roman Catholicism

The Roman Catholic Church's polity is hierarchical and probably the most centralized of religious bodies. Bishops are the ruling authorities in their diocese, overseeing individual parishes served by one or more clergy, but they are subject to the pope, who has primacy among the bishops. Papal teaching takes various forms (encyclicals, declarations, instructions, apostolic letters, and sermons), each having different authority. Generally speaking, papal teaching on matters of faith and morals is considered binding upon Catholics.

The Roman Catholic Church has a long history of theological reflection on matters relating to death and dying. That tradition reflects a consistent opposition to the direct ending of human life, whether at the beginning or end, though it was probably the earliest proponent of the moral justifiability of forgoing various forms of life-sustaining treatment.

The Catholic tradition forbids assisted suicide. The most recent authoritative statement of the church is the Sacred Congregation for the Doctrine of the Faith's 1980 *Declaration on Euthanasia*, issued with the approval of Pope John Paul II. While this document does not have the weight of an encyclical (the most authoritative pronouncement), it is morally binding on Catholics. Regarding assisted suicide, the document states:

> Intentionally causing one's own death, or suicide, is therefore equally wrong as murder. Such an action on the part of a person is a rejection of God's sovereignty and loving plan. Furthermore, suicide is also often a refusal of love for self, the denial of the natural instinct to live, a flight from the duties of justice and charity owed to one's neighbor, to various communities, or to the whole of society—although, as is generally recognized, at times there are psychological factors that can diminish responsibility or even completely remove it. (Congregation for the Doctrine of the Faith 1980)

The Vatican declaration also states:

> It is necessary to state firmly once more that nothing and no one can in any way permit the killing of an innocent human being, whether fetus or an embryo, an infant or an adult, an old person, or one suffering from an incurable disease, or a person who is dying. Furthermore, no one can request this act of killing, either for himself or herself or for another person entrusted to his or her care, nor can he or she

consent to it, either explicitly or implicitly. Nor can any authority legitimately recommend or permit such an action. For it is a question of the violation of the divine law, an offense against the dignity of the human person, a crime against life, and an attack on humanity. (CDF 1980)

At least three recent statements by the current pope reiterate this opposition to euthanasia (John Paul II, 1984; 1995: nos. 64-66; see also National Conference of Catholic Bishops 1994: no. 60; and *Catechism of the Catholic Church* 1994: nos. 2276-83).

## Islam

The authoritative sources of Islamic doctrines and practice are the Qur'an (Allah's revelations to the Prophet Muhammad, the basis for Muslim law and theology as well as for the principles and institutions of public life) and the Sunna (precepts and actions of the Prophet Muhammad not found in the Qur'an). According to Muslim beliefs, death occurs at God's will. There is no direct and explicit text in the Qur'an on euthanasia or assisted suicide, but there are texts that prohibit the taking of Muslim life. "Do not kill yourselves" (4:29) might mean "do not kill each other," but it also is an injunction against suicide, and in turn, is interpreted to mean that a Muslim killing another Muslim is tantamount to killing oneself. According to Islamic law, God is creator of life; therefore, a person does not "own" his or her life and hence cannot terminate it or ask another to take it (see Haleem 1993:16). It is an obligation of society to relieve the person of pain, but life is sacred (5:32). Since medical practice serves the will of God:

[The] doctor is well advised to realize his limit and not transgress it. If it is scientifically certain that life cannot be restored, then it is futile to diligently [maintain] the vegetative state of the patient by heroic means of animation or preserve him . . . [by] artificial means. It is the process of life that the doctor aims to maintain and not the process of dying. In any case, the doctor shall not take a positive measure to terminate the patient's life. (First International Conference on Islamic Medicine 1981)

## Adventist (Seventh-day)

The overall administrative body of the Seventh-day Adventist church is the executive committee of the general conference, which meets every five years. The general body is made up the "local conferences," of which there are 413. Each has a great deal of autonomy and supervises all local and pastoral work.

In October 1992, a consensus statement regarding physician-assisted suicide was approved at the Annual Council session in Silver Spring, Maryland. Seventh-day Adventists maintain an explicit distinction between "letting die" and physician-assisted suicide:

> Seventh-day Adventists believe that allowing a patient to die by forgoing medical interventions that only prolong suffering and postpone the moment of death is morally different from actions that have as their primary intention the direct taking of a life. (*What We Believe* 1992, p. 2)

In addition, Seventh-day Adventists point to scripture (Genesis 9:5-6; Exodus 20:13; 23:7) to justify their position. They feel that "while Christian love may lead to the withholding or withdrawing of medical interventions that only increase suffering or prolong dying," they do not "practice mercy killing or assist in suicide" (p. 3). Thus, Seventh-day Adventists oppose any legislation that condones physician-assisted suicide.

## Baptist Churches

There are more than thirty Baptist denominations in the United States, reflecting a tradition of independence and theological diversity. Baptists emphasize the complete autonomy of the individual congregation as well as freedom of thought and expression. There is no central authority, though Baptists do organize into local, state, and regional associations and hold national conventions to discuss common concerns and facilitate the achievement of common goals. It is not surprising that there is no "official" position of the Baptist churches regarding physician-assisted suicide, though individual denominations have taken positions.

The Southern Baptist Convention, organized in 1845, is the largest Baptist denomination. The SBC adamantly affirms "the biblical prohibition against taking the innocent human life by another person, or oneself, through euthanasia or [physician-assisted suicide]" (Resolution No. 13, adopted 1992). In 1996 the SBC meeting reaffirmed its position against physician-assisted suicide, citing both scripture and the Hippocratic Oath to support the claim:

"Be it therefore resolved, that we the messengers of the Southern Baptist Convention, meeting in New Orleans, Louisiana, affirm the biblical and Hippocratic prohibitions against assisted suicide." The SBC "vigorously [denounces] assisted suicide as an appropriate means of treating suffering"

(Resolution No. 7).

The fourth largest denomination in the U. S., the American Baptists, in 1989 issued a "statement of concern" entitled "Death and Dying: Responsibilities and Choices." It offers guidelines for choices about one's own or another's dying and outlines the responsibilities of the individual, the family, health care professionals, and the church in this regard. The document primarily concerns decisions to forgo life-sustaining treatment "if no reasonable expectation exists for recovery."

The General Association of General Baptists opposes assisted suicide:

> We believe life and death belong in the hands of God. Regardless of circumstances that befall man, he must know that God gave him existence and He holds him responsible for his stewardship of life. . . . The deliberate termination of life is a serious concern, whether it is done by the person himself, a friend, or the physician. We oppose euthanasia, sometimes referred to as mercy killing. (Social Issues Commission 1989, p. 9)

None of the other large Baptist denominations—the National Baptist Convention of the U.S.A., the National Baptist Convention of America, the National Primitive Baptist Convention, or the Baptist Bible Fellowship—appears to have a formal position on physician-assisted suicide.

## Christian Church (Disciples of Christ)

Long a loosely bound association of local churches, the Disciples of Christ adopted a more centrally controlled and representative organizational structure at the 1968 gathering of the International Assembly. While the local congregation remained the basic unit, the churches were organized into thirty-five regions, each with its own board and committees. A general assembly meets every two years. In the interim, a general board and its administrative committee deal with matters of church life.

The Christian Church (Disciples of Christ) began passing resolutions on moral issues at its general assemblies in the 1970s. Still, this activity did not diminish the church's long tradition of liberty of conscience, as the *Handbook for Today's Disciples* (Cummins 1981) notes:

> If you ask about the moral correctness of having an abortion, the appropriate expression of human sexuality, seeking a divorce, consuming drugs or participating in any number of other activities which raise questions of an ethical or moral nature, the Christian Church (Disciples of Christ) will not provide a systematic blueprint for your personal behavior.

The denomination's tradition of personal moral liberty is very strong:

> While Disciples as a body may disapprove of the general practice of abortion they recognize a greater danger of legislating a single moral opinion for all persons, thereby abridging the freedom of individual choice. On moral ethical questions related to personal behavior, Disciples tend to affirm and reaffirm this position which is cherished as part of their heritage.

Thus, the only action related to physician-assisted suicide taken by the Christian Church (Disciples of Christ) is a resolution approved by the 1977 General Assembly calling for a study of issues related to dying with dignity, development of a theological statement on the matter to assist members, and participation in public policy discussions to underscore the moral issues.

## Christian Science

A five-person board of directors in Boston administers the Church of Christ, Scientist, though local churches enjoy their own forms of democratic government. Generally, the board does not establish official positions on social and personal issues. Church members are free to follow their consciences.

Christian Science belief in the power of God to heal, however, has significant bearing on physician-assisted suicide because Christian Scientists rely on spiritual means for healing. They accept as fact the biblical stories of Jesus curing diseases that were considered incurable and expecting his followers to do the same.

A Christian Scientist does not consider any disease to be beyond the power of God to heal. For this reason, Christian Scientists are not advocates of physician-assisted suicide (Larue 1985, 114-115).

## Episcopal Church

The church's form of government consists of a federation of dioceses, each autonomous and under the administration of a bishop. Each diocese is represented at an annual diocesan convention and at a triennial General Convention. The Episcopal Church requires unity in essentials of doctrine, discipline, and worship but allows for considerable variation, individuality, and autonomy in moral matters. Even official resolutions of the General Convention are not juridically binding on Episcopalians.

The 1991 General Convention affirms that it is morally wrong and unacceptable "to intentionally take a human life in order to relieve the suffering caused by incurable illness. This would include the intentional shortening of another person's life by the use of a lethal dose of medication or poison, the use of lethal weapons, homicidal acts, and other forms of [physician-assisted suicide]" (Journal of the General Convention 1991:AO93a, no. 1, p. 383). However, a proposed amendment to this guideline affirms that "palliative treatment to relieve the pain of persons with progressive incurable illnesses, even if done with the knowledge that a hastened death may result, is consistent with the theological tenets regarding the sanctity of life" (General Convention of the Episcopal Church 1994:AO56).

## Jehovah's Witness

The Jehovah's Witness publication, *Awake!*, summarizes the tradition's views on physician-assisted suicide. Jehovah's Witnesses reject physician-assisted suicide for several reasons. First, it violates the commandment prohibiting murder (Exodus 20:13). Second, it violates the biblical command that Christians "hold a good conscience" (1 Peter 3:16). For Jehovah's Witnesses, this passage refers to the medical profession's general injunction against taking active measures to hasten a patient's death. Finally, Christians must "be in subjection to superior authorities" (Romans 12:1) and obey the law of the land.

The Bible shows that God views human life as something sacred (Genesis 9:6; Psalms 36:9). Thus, Jehovah's Witnesses believe, a Christian conscientiously could not become party to a mercy killing even if a person is suffering greatly from illness (Watch Tower Bible Tract Society of New York, Inc. August 12, 1998).

In some instances, Jehovah's Witnesses do not oppose forgoing life-sustaining treatment. Moreover, they see no scriptural basis for prolonging the dying process for a person who is terminally ill (Ibid.)

### Latter-day Saints (Mormon Church)

The Mormon president and two counselors make up the presiding council of the Mormon Church. This group has final and universal authority over both spiritual and temporal affairs. The president is considered to be the "mouthpiece of God," and the receiver of church law through direct revelation.

With regard to euthanasia and assisted suicide, the Mormon church maintains the following policy: "A person who participates in euthanasia—deliberately putting to death a person suffering from incurable conditions or diseases—violates the commandments of God" (*1989 General Handbook*, 11-5).

### Lutheran Churches

Decision-making in the Lutheran Church–Missouri Synod devolves on delegates to regional and national conventions. Triennial General Conventions of pastors and laypeople choose directors for the church body.

The Lutheran Church-Missouri Synod adamantly opposes physician-assisted suicide. In 1993 the Commission on Theology and Church Relations released an updated version

of the 1979 *Report on Euthanasia with Guiding Principles.*
This report affirms the church's opposition to physician-assisted suicide:

> To the dismay and fear of many, the advocates of euthanasia, as well as assisted suicide, have sought to justify the taking of human life on moral grounds by describing it as a truly compassionate act aimed at the relief of human suffering. In the light of what Scriptures say about the kind of care God wills that we provide to those who suffer and are facing death, we reject such claims as neither compassionate nor caring. Christians aim always to care, never to kill (Lutheran Church-Missouri Synod 1993, p. 3).

In 1988 the American Lutheran Church, the Lutheran Church in America, and the Association of Evangelical Lutheran Churches merged to form the Evangelical Lutheran Church in America (ELCA). In 1992 the ELCA Church Council of the newly formed church convened to address the issue of physician-assisted suicide. While the ELCA officially forbids "the deliberate action of a physician to take the life of a patient," it does recognize the often-complex ambiguities surrounding this issue (ELCA 1992, p. 4). Often the health care provider must choose between preserving the life and health of the patient and relieving pain.

> As a church, we affirm that deliberately destroying life created in the image of God is contrary to our Christian conscience. While this affirmation is clear, we also recognize that responsible health care professionals struggle to choose the lesser evil in ambiguous borderline situations—for example,

when pain becomes so unmanageable that life is indistinguishable from torture. (ELCA 1992, p. 4)

However, the ELCA vigorously rejects the legalization of assisted suicide, asking if it is ever morally permissible for a physician deliberately to act or authorize an action to terminate the life of a patient.

The denomination opposes the legalization of physician-assisted death, which would allow the private killing of one person by another. Public control and regulation of such actions would be extremely difficult, if not impossible. The potential for abuse, especially of people who are most vulnerable, would be substantially increased.

## United Methodist Church

Methodism is a highly organized religious body. The quadrennial General Conference, composed of bishops and lay representatives, is the lawmaking body of the church. Proposals adopted by the General Conference become Methodist law. Implementation is carried out by a variety of boards and agencies. Having said this, however, it important to note that the Methodist church has not developed an institutional tradition of reflection on the moral nature of specific medical interventions.

The United Methodist Church cautiously recognizes the appeal of physician-assisted suicide. The 1996 *Book of Resolutions of the United Methodist Church* notes, "Some persons confronted with a terminal illness, that promises prolonged suffering and anguish for themselves and for loved ones, may consider suicide as a means to hasten death" (p. 3). However, the church suggests that while "suicide may be the humane solution for the problem of excruciating pain experienced by the terminally ill," this option "is minimized by effective medical management of pain" (p. 4).

Therefore, the denomination encourages methods of controlling pain, "even when they risk or shorten life," and "provided the intention is to relieve pain and not to kill" (p. 5).

## Reformed-Presbyterian

The regional governing body of this church, composed of equal numbers of clergy and laity as well as the ruling body of each local church, is called a "presbytery." Several regional presbyteries may form a synod, and synods form the largest body known as the General Assembly, which meets annually.

While the Reformed tradition emphasizes the value that God places on life, it does not necessarily regard assisted suicide or euthanasia as inconsistent with respect for life:

Presbyterians make a distinction between "active" euthanasia, where death may not be assumed, and "passive" euthanasia, where death is predictable and depends on whether medical interventions are made and continued. They do not rule out either active or passive euthanasia in every case, but in all cases, for example, such as abortion or cancer, decisions must be made in terms of the value God places on life and the respect that Christians should have for life, and with pastoral concern for those making decisions about life and death. Although dying may have its sting, it is, from the Christian perspective . . . not the last word about the value of life. (Smylie 1986:233)

## Unitarian Universalist Association

The Association's constitution establishes a general assembly as the overall policy-making body for carrying out the purposes and objectives of the association. It generally meets annually.

In the statement "The Right to Die with Dignity," the 1988 Unitarian Universalist General Assembly made several statements in support of physician-assisted suicide. It affirmed that the dignity of human life may be compromised when life is extended beyond the will or ability of a person to sustain that dignity. Prolongation of life may cause unnecessary suffering and loss of dignity while providing little or nothing of benefit to the individual. Therefore, the Assembly supported the right to self-determination in dying and the release from civil or criminal penalties of those who, under proper safeguards, act to honor the right of terminally ill patients to select the time of their own deaths. The Assembly strongly advocated safeguards against abuses by those who would hasten death contrary to the individual's desires. Finally, it urged Unitarians to petition legislators to support legislation that will create legal protection for the right to die with dignity, in accordance with one's own choice (General Assembly of Unitarian Universalists 1988, 74).

## United Church of Christ

The United Church of Christ is the result of the 1957 merger of two denominations, the Congregational Christian Churches (born of the 1931 merger of the Congregational Churches and the Christian Churches) and the Evangelical and Reformed Church (which was the 1934 merger of the General Synod of the Reformed Churches in the United States and the Evangelical Church of North America). The UCC organizes its local congregations into associations (geographic groupings of local churches that meet annually), conferences (regional groupings of associations), and the General Synod, which meets biennially. The synod is the top representative body of the church and establishes the various boards, commissions, and councils that oversee the work of the church as a whole.

During its brief history, the UCC has gained a reputation for taking progressive stands on matters of social policy—particularly through the actions of its General Synod. But, contrary to many other Christian denominations, the actions of the UCC's General Synod are not binding for other bodies of the church. This is because the General Synod speaks to others within the denomination and to the wider society in an advisory rather than a determinative way. This is why the actions of the General Synod are not necessarily embraced by all of its constituents and why deference is tolerated—even expected—within the United Church of Christ.

In June 1990 the Rocky Mountain Conference—a regional body of the United Church of Christ—adopted a resolution, "The Rights and Responsibilities of Christians Regarding Human Death," which supported the rights of individuals and families to make decisions regarding human death and dying. As part of this resolution, the UCC churches within the Rocky Mountain Conference affirmed the right of persons under hopeless and irreversible conditions to terminate their lives and emphasized that "Christian understanding and compassion are appropriate with regard to suicide and euthanasia." The Conference further encouraged legislation to safeguard this right, including the rights of those who are unable to make decisions for themselves. The Rocky Mountain Conference presented its resolution to the Eighteenth General Synod in 1991, which did not endorse it.

## Eastern Orthodoxy

As with Western branches of Christianity, the Eastern Orthodox Church is the result of the "great schism" between Eastern and Western Christianity that occurred in 1054 C.E. with the mutual excommunication of the pope of Rome and the patriarch of Constantinople. The pope remained head of the Western church, but the Eastern church developed national, autonomous sees organized around the office and person of the bishop. There are four modern patriarchates (Russia, Serbia, Romania, and Bulgaria) and a number of self-governing churches. The patriarchs have equal authority and no jurisdiction in each other's see. They are, however, in communion with each other. Sources of Eastern Orthodox ethics are scripture and tradition—the "mind of the church," as discerned in the decisions of ecumenical and local councils, the writings of the Fathers of the Church, and canon law. In the United States, the Greek and Russian Orthodox churches are the two largest Eastern Orthodox churches.

The Greek Orthodox Church does not permit its members to take direct action to shorten a person's life for any reason. To do this is to usurp a prerogative that is God's alone. It therefore is a form of murder, which is a serious sin. On the other hand, the tradition does not oblige its members to prolong unnecessarily the dying process through elaborate technical efforts (see Harakas 1982, 171).

Responding to a questionnaire on the moral permissibility of euthanasia within the Russian Orthodox tradition, the Very Reverend Archpriest A. Mileant of Protection of the Holy Virgin Russian Orthodox Church in Los Angeles made the following statement:

We consider that human life is a gift of God, which no one has the right to forcibly take away. . . . If a person is in great pain and requests to be allowed to die sooner (or his relatives so request), we do not consider it possible to accede to his request, because we believe that suffering is often sent by God for the remission of our sins and the salvation of our souls; so if God has sent someone pain which cannot be alleviated by normal means (painkiller shots, etc.), we must resign ourselves in the knowledge that this pain is necessary and inevitable. (Larue 1985, 56-57)

## Hinduism

Hindu medical ethics are embedded in ancient and diverse medical and cultural traditions. Unlike Western countries, where modern medical technologies have fostered new concerns with the ethics of hastening death, medicine in India continues to be largely indigenous, and as such ethical concerns with assisted suicide are more consistent with the classical and folk religious traditions. Since Hinduism has no universally accepted scripture or priestly hierarchy, the code of ethics for human conduct has always been flexible and subject to local interpretation. Of particular importance, therefore, in a discussion of Hindu views on assisted suicide are the shared concepts of dharma and karma.

Although Hinduism's diversity makes it difficult to formulate moral imperatives that are binding for all, there is a great respect and concern for continuity and order epitomized by the concept of dharma, that which sustains and holds people together individually and collectively (Desai 1989, 18-21). Dharma is the law of morality or ethics; adherence to that law is an obligation through which believers secure well-being now and later, after death. It establishes moral norms and expectations for every aspect of life. One's actions, feelings, and attitudes toward death, for instance, are guided by the traditions and structures of dharma that have evolved through the centuries.

Central to the theory of rebirth and the causality of life, karma is fundamental to an understanding of Hindu attitudes toward assisted suicide. Dharma assigns actions or duties, and karma holds a person to them. Thus morality inherent in every human action has a potential for immediate or eventual reward or punishment. One cannot alter that which has already been done, but the present and future offer opportunities for modifying one's fate. By this logic, life events imply antecedent actions that can be played out over multiple lifetimes. Karmic laws are invoked generally when unforeseen and undesirable developments like grave illness or chronic disability occur. The pain and suffering of terminal illness, for example, are the consequences of past actions. How one faces illness, disability, or death will help determine the conditions of the next or future lives.

The ethical problems encountered at death are relatively simple. Death does produce anxieties in the dying and feelings of sorrow and loss in survivors, but for the various traditions within Hinduism, death is not the opposite of life; it is the opposite of birth. Each event marks a passage. In time everyone must die when the body is worn out and when one has paid the accumulated debt of karma. What is mourned is an untimely or premature death, for the unsatisfied debt from a past life is carried over into the next one. Death may come as a relief from physical suffering that reduces quality of life, and one can take solace in the expectation of rebirth. A person should be allowed to die peacefully, for artificially sustained life is of little value.

Generally, there was an early reluctance to endorse any form of self-willed death, given the prescription of living out a natural life span and the obligations of karma. While the prohibition against suicide was strong, some religious lawgivers (Brahmins) sought to define the biological, psychological, and social conditions for an acceptable rationale under which suicide could be condoned in highly selected circumstances, for instance, under conditions of extreme old age or severe or terminal illness.

The *Dharmasastra* literature, which outlines Hindu codes of conduct, also refers to a form of religious suicide, justified by incurable disease or great misfortune, when one can no longer perform the rites of bodily purification (Kane 1974, 2:926). These duties are required by one's dharma, the law of morality to which believers must adhere and through which they secure well-being now and later, after death. Failing to perform dharma carries karmic consequences. Since incapacitated people cannot perform mandatory, religious duties because of their circumstances, exceptions for them must be created. Under these circumstances, assisted suicide as a form of euthanasia (self-willed and self-accomplished, with the aid of another) may be considered acceptable.

## Buddhism

Buddhism reflects a tremendous doctrinal, liturgical, and organizational diversity, largely the result of geographical diffusion and cultural adaptation. As the teachings of Siddhartha Gautama, the Buddha (ca. 563-483 B.C.E.)

spread through India into Southeast and Central Asia, Tibet, China, Korea, and Japan, Buddhism developed into a number of movements, schools, and sects. As a result, it is not surprising that there is no official position regarding physician-assisted suicide. In the midst of its variety, some common doctrinal features provide ethical guidance on assisted suicide as a form of euthanasia.

The final goal of Buddhist practice is enlightenment, the transforming and liberating insight into the nature of reality. In the quest for enlightenment, all Buddhists undergo three-fold training in ethics, meditation, and wisdom. There is a substantial Buddhist literature dealing with ethical or moral issues within its many schools of thought. However, the fundamental basis of all Buddhist ethics is found in the ten precepts or teachings about veracity, justice, and compassion, the first of which states that a Buddhist should refrain from destroying life. Death should never be directly willed either as a means or an end.

Along with this fundamental respect for life, two central concepts are essential to understanding a Buddhist view of assisted suicide, namely, rebirth and karma. According to the Buddhist doctrine of rebirth, one has had countless past lifetimes and faces countless future lives until *samsara* (the wheel of rebirth) is ended by enlightenment. Buddhist cosmology posits six realms of existence for sentient being; karma determines the realm through which one transmigrates. Of these six realms, the most beneficial form is that of the human being. However, its attainment is the most difficult; thus it is highly prized and to be protected. Buddhism therefore upholds the sanctity of all human life regardless of its condition.

The doctrine of karma maintains a correlation between action and consequence. According to this doctrine, each person's condition, with its particular joys and sorrows, is nothing more or less than the result of his or her past actions, good or bad (Ratanakal 1988:301-12). In Buddhism all illness and death have their origins in karma, which has its origins in ignorance about the true nature of reality. In some lifetime, when the person achieves understanding of that reality, karma will no longer be accrued, suffering will end, and rebirth will occur no more. A Buddhist might argue that assisted suicide or mercy killing to forestall pain and suffering is misguided, contributing to the perpetuation of karma and rebirth.

Thus a terminal illness represents the repayment of a karmic debt. If the complete evolution of the debt were to be disrupted by an active intervention by a physician, it would need to be faced again in a future existence. Indeed, since human existence is so difficult to obtain, a person whose life was prematurely ended by suicide or euthanasia might have to endure the same ripening karma in a disadvantageous realm of existence. Thus it would be better to confront the results of one's past actions in the current lifetime with spiritual teachers, family, and health professionals.

While Buddhism regards life as a basic good, it does not follow that it is something that must be preserved at all costs. Death is a natural part of the *samsaric* circle and must be accepted as such. It is not the final end but the doorway to rebirth. This recognition allows for the withholding or withdrawal of medical treatment that serves no useful purpose. Thus, there is no obligation for physicians to keep a patient alive at all costs. In the case of elderly or terminal cases, it is far more important to assist patients in developing the right mental attitude toward death than attempting to postpone it or act to cause it (see Gyatso 1982, 67-68; Keown 1995, 186-187).

# CHAPTER FOUR

# CONCLUSION

■ ■ □

As the various states debate the justifiability and social acceptability of physician-assisted suicide, individuals and communities have the opportunity to address constructively and creatively some of the most fundamental issues surrounding how we care for those who die. As legislators and policy makers struggle to meet the challenge of assisted suicide, religious traditions will have a crucial role to play. Everyone would do well to take care in framing the debate and making any hasty resolutions.

For many, the public debate about physician-assisted suicide may not only be a serious breach of social taboo but a vicious attack on the value of human life. Such people will likely frame their response to the debate in "right to life" language. Others may consider assisted suicide to be the culmination of efforts to achieve greater autonomy over one's life. These people will likely frame their response to the debate in the "right to die" language. Rather than draw battle lines, we should embrace the opportunity for a richer, deeper, more fruitful debate.

We hope that this handbook has offered a sense of the complexity of the issue. Rarely is an opinion as simple as being for or against physician-assisted suicide; nor can the debate be reduced to the right to life vs. the right to die, negative consequences vs. positive consequences, slippery slope arguments vs. their rejection. These factors undoubtedly have their place in the discussion, but to remain focused on them is to ignore deeper issues.

We currently care for the dying with highly technological, cure-oriented medicine. The fears and difficulties generated by this approach are real and need to be reckoned with. Most people agree that it would be shortsighted at best to opt for physician-assisted dying before we have made a serious attempt to change the factors contributing to a desire for such a death. In other words, we should not disregard the troubling aspects of current attitudes and practices toward dying because all our attention has turned toward PAS.

There are yet other, more profound issues to be addressed that often go unexamined in public policy debates about the legalization of PAS. These issues may be clustered under the umbrella of "core beliefs." People hold convictions about human nature, the ultimate purposes of life, and the meaning of pain, suffering, finitude, dependency, and death. These beliefs shape how individuals perceive and experience illness, healing, dying, and other fundamental human realities. Whether suffering, for example, is seen as an unmitigated evil to be eliminated in any way possible, as punishment, as formative of the self, or as somehow redemptive will depend to a considerable degree on one's view of the purpose of human existence. Death may be seen, among other things, as an absurd annihilation of human experience and achievement, the culmination of one's lifelong process of self-creation, deliverance from this earthly journey, or passage to a destiny beyond life. If the debate about PAS is not rushed or narrowed to a debate about rights and consequences, it could provide the opportunity for reexamining a host of relevant core beliefs.

Religious traditions have a crucial role to play in this connection. Seeking the meaning of life's most fundamental human experiences brings one to the threshold of the religious, and religious traditions have a long and rich history of interpreting these realities. Many traditions are still searching for ways to speak to our secular, technological culture, and the PAS debate opens up opportunities for communication between the two, opportunities that, it is hoped, will be marked by openness and honesty.

It may be time for American society to come to terms with the notion of autonomy, particularly as it bears upon public policy. Central to the physician-assisted suicide debate is the relation of the individual to the community. In recent years, an increasing chorus of voices has been questioning the sacrosanct status of individual autonomy in the United States. Critics perceive the problem as lying not so much with autonomy as with its scope, its limits, and its frequent neglect of responsibilities to other individuals, society as a whole, and the common good. Probing the appropriateness and wisdom of a public policy permitting physician-assisted suicide could provide space for a much-needed debate about the underlying presuppositions in our democratic, capitalist society.

# FOR MORE INFORMATION REGARDING PHYSICIAN-ASSISTED SUICIDE AND CARE OF THE DYING

Agency for Health Care Policy and Research
301-594-4015

The American Academy of Hospice and Palliative Care
703-787-7718

American College of Physicians
800-523-1546

Americans for Better Care of the Dying
202-530-9864

American Geriatrics Society
212-308-1414

American Medical Association
312-464-5000

American Nurses Association
202-651-7000

American Pain Society
847-375-4715

American Society of Law, Medicine, and Ethics
617-262-4990

Americans for Better Care of the Dying
202-530-9864

Center to Improve Care of the Dying
202-467-2222

Choice in Dying
800-989-9455

Compassion in Dying Federation
503-221-9556

Federation of State Medical Boards
817-868-4000

Hawaii Blue Ribbon Panel on Living and Dying with Dignity
808-586-7309

The Hemlock Society
800-247-7421

Illinois Task Force on Comfort Care for the Terminally Ill
217-259-6173

Maine Coalition for Dialogue on Death and Dying
207-729-3602

Maryland Attorney General's Project on Care at the End of Life
410-576-6327

Midwest Bioethics Center
816-221-1100

Missoula Demonstration Project
406-728-1613

National Association of Social Workers
202-408-8600

National Conference of State Legislatures
Health Policy Tracking Service
202-624-3567
Forum for State Health Policy Leadership
202-624-3580

National Hospice Organization
703-243-5900

National Right to Life Committee
202-626-8800

Nevada Attorney General's Office Death with Dignity Project
702-688-1822

New York State Attorney General's Office
Commission on Quality Care at the End of Life
212-416-8095

New York State Task Force on Life and the Law
212-613-4303

Oregon Death with Dignity Legal Defense and Education Center
503-228-6079

Oregon Health Sciences Center
Center for Ethics in Health Care
503-494-4466

Project on Death in America
212-247-3890

The Robert Wood Johnson Foundation
Last Acts Campaign
http://www.lastacts.org

National Program Office
Community-State Partnerships to Improve End-of-Life Care
816-842-7110

Task Force to Improve the Care of Terminally Ill Oregonians
503-413-7997

Vermont Medical Society Palliative Care Initiative
802-223-7898

# REFERENCES

"Americans say, 'Keep your laws off my body.'" 1999.
*Medical Ethics Advisor* 15, 5 (May): 52-53.

Back, et al. 1996.
"Physician-Assisted Suicide and Euthanasia in Washington
State." *Journal of the American Medical Association* 275 (March
27): 919-25.

Battin, Margaret. 1994.
*The Least Worst Death: Essays in Bioethics on the End of Life.*
New York: Oxford University Press.

––. 1996.
*The Death Debate: Ethical Issues in Suicide.* Upper Saddle River,
Nj.: Prentice-Hall.

Canady, Charles T. 1998.
"Physician-Assisted Suicide and Euthanasia in the Netherlands: A Report to the House Judiciary Subcommittee on the Constitution." *Issues in Law and Medicine* 14, no. 3 (Winter): 301-324.

*Catechism of the Catholic Church.* 1994.
New York: Doubleday.

Chin, Arthur et al. 1999.
"Legalized Physician-Assisted Suicide in Oregon–The First Year's Experience." *The New England Journal of Medicine* 340 (February 18): 577-83.

Church of Jesus Christ of Latter-day Saints. 1989.
Public Affairs Department. *The General Handbook of Instruction of the Church of Jesus Christ of Latter-day Saints.* The Handbook is for leaders of the church at the general and local levels.

Congregation for the Doctrine of the Faith. 1980.
*Declaration on Euthanasia.*

Covinsky, Kenneth et al. 1996.
"Is Economic Hardship on the Families of the Seriously Ill Associated with Patient and Surrogate Care Preferences?" *Archives of Internal Medicine* 156(1): 737-1, 741.

Cummins, D. Duane. 1981. *A Handbook for Today's Disciples.* St. Louis, Mo.

Desai, Prakash. 1988. "Medical Ethics in India." *Journal of Philosophy and Medicine* 13 (August): 231-55.

——. 1989.
*Health and Medicine in the Hindu Tradition.* New York: Crossroad.

Dorf, Michael, and Colb, Sherry, Counsel of Record. 1996.
Excerpted from BRIEF AMICUS CURIAE OF STATE LEGISLATORS IN SUPPORT OF RESPONDENTS in Vacco vs. Quill, Nos. 95-1858, and Washington vs. Glucksberg, Nos. 96-110, available at press time on the University of Pennsylvania

bioethics.net website,
http://www.med.upenn.edu/bioethics/index.shtml

Dorff, Elliot. 1991.
"A Jewish Approach to End-Stage Medical Care." *Conservative Judaism* 43, 3 (Spring): 3-51.

The Ethics and Religious Life Commission of the Southern Baptist Convention. Resolution no. 13 adopted 1992; resolution no. 7 adopted 1996.

Evangelical Lutheran Church in America, Church Council of the ELCA. 1992.
*End of Life Decisions* Chicago: Division for Church in Society.

Feldman, David, and Fred Rosner, eds. 1984.
*Compendium on Medical Ethics*; 6th ed. New York: Federation of Jewish Philanthropies of New York.

Fenigson, Richard. 1991.
"The Report of the Dutch Governmental Committee on Euthanasia." *Issues in Law and Medicine* 7 (Winter): 339ff.

First International Conference on Islamic Medicine. 1981. *Islamic Code of Medical Ethics*. Kuwait Document, Kuwait Rabi I, 1401 (January).

General Assembly of Unitarian Universalists.
*1988 Proceedings*.

General Convention of the Episcopal Church. 1994.
*The Blue Book: Reports of the Committees, Commissions, Boards, and Agencies of the General Convention of the Episcopal Church, 1994*. New York: Episcopal Church Center.

Gest, T. 1990.
"Changing the Rules on Dying." *US News and World Report* (July 9), pp. 22-24.

"Giving Death a Hand." 1990.
*New York Times* (June 14), p. A6.

Gyatso, S. 1982.
  *Essence of Refined Gold.* Trans. and ed., G. H. Mullin. Ithaca,
  NY.: Gabriel/Snow Lion.

Haleem, M. A. S. Abdel. 1993.
  "Medical Ethics in Islam," In A. Grubb, ed. *Choices and Decisions in Health Care.* 14-20.New York: John Wiley & Sons.

Hamel, Ron, ed. 1991.
  *Choosing Death: Active Euthanasia, Religion, and the Public
  Debate.* Philadelphia: Trinity Press.

Harakas, Stanley S. 1988
  *The Orthodox Church: 455 Questions and Answers* (1988). Minneapolis, Mn.: Light and Life Publications.

––. 1982.
  *Contemporary Moral Issues.* Minneapolis, Mn.: Light and Life
  Publications.

The Hemlock Society. 1991.
  *Roper Poll of the West Coast on Euthanasia.* New York: The
  Roper Organization.

Humber, James M., Robert Almeder, and Gregg Kasting. 1993.
  *Physician-Assisted Death.* Totowa, NJ.: Humana Press.

John Paul II. 1984.
  "Opposing Euthanasia"

––. 1985.
  "The Mystery of Life and Death"

––. 1995.
  "The Gospel of Life" (*Evangelium vitae*). New York: Random
  House.

*Journal of the General Convention of the Episcopal Church* (House
  of Bishops). 1991.

Kane, Pandurang Vaman. 1974.
  *A History of Dharmasastra: Ancient and Medieval Religious and*

*Civil Law in India*. Poona, India: Bhandarkar Oriental Research Institute.

Keisling, Phil. 1994.
*Official Abstract of Votes General Election*. Salem, OR.: State Elections Division (November 8): i, 54.

Keown, Damien. 1995.
*Buddhism & Bioethics*. London: St. Martin's Press.

LaRue, Gerald. 1985.
*Euthanasia and Religion: A Survey of the Attitudes of World Religions to the Right-to-Die*. Los Angeles: Hemlock Society.

Lee, M. A., et al. 1996.
"Legalizing Assisted Suicide—Views of Physicians in Oregon." *New England Journal of Medicine* 334 (Feb. 1): 310-15.

Lutheran Church–Missouri Synod, Commission on Theology and Church Relations, Social Concerns Committee. 1993.
*Christian Care at Life's End*.

May, William. 1996.
*Testing the Medical Covenant: Active Euthanasia and Health Care Reform*. Grand Rapids, Mi.: Eerdmans.

Meisel, Alan. 1999.
*The Right to Die*, 2nd ed. Cumulative supplement. New York: Wiley.

The Mennonite Church General Board. 1998.
"Physician-Assisted Suicide." (fax communication, Aug. 6).

Merritt, Pick, et al. 1998.
*State Initiatives in End-of-Life Care: Policy Guide for State Legislators*. Forum for State Health Policy Leadership and the Center to Improve Care of the Dying.

National Conference of Catholic Bishops. 1994.
*Ethical and Religious Directives for Catholic Health Care Services*. Washington, D.C.: United States Catholic Conference.

The New York State Task Force on Life and the Law. 1994.
*When Death is Sought: Assisted Suicide and Euthanasia in the Medical Context*. New York: The New York State Task Force on Life and the Law.

Quill, Timothy. 1991.
"Death and Dignity: A Case of Individualized Decision Making." *New England Journal of Medicine* 324, 10 (March 7): 691-94.

Ratanakal, Pinit. 1988.
"Bioethics in Thailand: The Struggle for Buddhist Solutions." *Journal of Medicine and Philosophy* 13 (August): 301-12.

Rosenbaum, David. 1996.
"Americans Want a Right to Die. Or So They Think." *The New York Times* (June 8).

Scitovsky, Anne. 1991.
" 'The High Cost of Dying' Revisited." *The Milbank Quarterly* 72(4):561-91.

Smylie, James. 1986.
"The Reformed Tradition," In Ronald Numbers and Darrel Amundsen, eds. *Caring and Curing: Health and Medicine in the Western Religious Traditions*. New York: Macmillan.

Social Issues Commission of the General Association of General Baptists. 1989.
*The Social Principles of General Baptists*. Poplar Bluff, Mo.: General Report of General Baptists.

Solomon, Mildred, et al. 1993.
"Decisions Near the End of Life: Professional Views on Life-Sustaining Treatments." *American Journal of Public Health* 83 (January):14-23.

Social Issues Commission of the General Association of General Baptists. 1989.
*The Social Principles of General Baptists*. Poplar Bluffs, Mo.: General Report of General Baptists.

"State of Assisted Suicide in the U.S." 1999.
*Medical Ethics Advisor* 15 (May):49-60.

The SUPPORT Principal Investigators. 1995.
"A Controlled Trial to Improve Care for Seriously Ill Hospitalized Patients: The Study to Understand Prognoses and Preferences for Outcomes and Treatments (SUPPORT)." *Journal of the American Medical Association* 274(2): 1591-1598.

The Task Force to Improve the Care of Terminally-Ill Oregonians. 1998.
*The Oregon Death With Dignity Act: A Guidebook for Health Care Providers.* The Center for Ethics in Health Care, Oregon Health Sciences University, Portland, Or.

Vacco v. Quill. No. 117 S.Ct. 2293 (1997).

Van der Maas, Paul, et al. 1992.
"Euthanasia and Other Medical Decisions Concerning the End of Life: An Investigation Performed upon Request of the Commission of Inquiry into the Medical Practice Concerning Euthanasia." *Health Policy* 22, Nos. 1 and 2 [Hereafter Remmelink Report].
In contrast, there are no reliable figures on how many physician-assisted suicides take place in the United States, where approximately two-and-a-half million people die each year.

Watch Tower Bible Tract Society of New York, Inc. (August) 1998.

Washington v. Glucksberg. No. 117 S. Ct. 2258 (1997).

Webb, Marilyn. 1997.
*The Good Death: The New American Search to Reshape the End of Life* New York: Bantam Books.

Weir, Robert. ed. 1997.
*Physician-Assisted Suicide.* Bloomington, In: Indiana University Press.

*What We Believe* 1998.
E-mail statement; see www.adventist.org.

# APPENDIX A

# DEATH WITH DIGNITY PROPOSALS

At least eight states have considered adoption of legislation patterned after Oregon's "Death with Dignity Act," Or. Rev. Stat. §§ 127.800 et seq (1995). States in which the legislation has been proposed include the following:

ARIZONA – S.B. 1007.
> Introduced January 8, 1996; to committee January 16, 1996.

CALIFORNIA – S.B. 1310 and A.B. 1080.
> Introduced February 23, 1995; died in committee, January 31, 1996.

COLORADO – H.B. 1185-96.

Introduced January 1, 1996; referred to committee; action postponed indefinitely, February 2, 1996.

MAINE – H.P. 552.

Introduced March 7, 1995; House Committee on Judiciary votes not to recommend passage on June 14, 1995.

MASSACHUSETTS – H.B. 3173.

Introduced February 14, 1995.

NEW HAMPSHIRE – H.B. 339.

Introduced January 5, 1995; failed in House, January 4, 1996.

MISSISSIPPI – H.B. 1023.

Introduced January 22, 1996; died in committee February 6, 1996.

VERMONT – H.B. 335.

Introduced February 21, 1995.

These bills would have allowed competent adults suffering from terminal illness to request a self-administered lethal dosage of medication; authorized physicians to prescribe a lethal dose; set forth safeguards, procedures, immunities, and liabilities with respect to fulfilling such a request; and made voluntary the provision of aid in dying by hospital or physician. They would not have authorized active euthanasia, lethal injection, or mercy killing (Dorf and Colb, 1996).

## ADDITIONAL PROPOSALS AND ENACTMENTS

Other state legislators have introduced legislation to broaden laws regarding assisted suicide.

ALASKA – H.B. 371, introduced January 8, 1996, would
allow a competent adult suffering from terminal illness to
request self-administered lethal dosage of medication, and
authorize physician to prescribe lethal dose. Does not
authorize active euthanasia, lethal injection, or mercy
killing.

MARYLAND – H.B. 474, introduced January 31, 1996,
would, *inter alia*, allow a mentally competent adult suffering from a painful terminal condition to request aid in
dying, set forth procedures and safeguards for carrying out
such requests, and make participation in aid in dying
optional for physicians and hospitals.

MICHIGAN – H.B. 4134, introduced, January 17, 1996,
would allow qualified patients to make revocable request
for aid in dying, defined here as "provision of a lethal
agent"; create judicial review of aid-in-dying requests and
revocations; create immunities for those who provide aid-
in-dying.

NEW YORK – S.B. 5024 was introduced on May 3, 1995.
S.B. 5024 is in the Senate Committee on Health as of January 3, 1996. It would allow competent adult suffering
from terminal illness to request self-administered lethal
dosage of medication; authorize physician to prescribe
lethal dose; establish safeguards and record-keeping procedures for fulfilling aid-in-dying requests; and make provision of aid in dying by hospital or physician voluntary.
The bill does not authorize active euthanasia, lethal injection, or mercy killing.

RHODE ISLAND – S. 2985, introduced February 6, 1996,
would authorize physicians to help competent adults suffering from terminal or intractable and unbearable illness

to obtain the medical means of suicide, and to assist patient in administration of such means.

WISCONSIN – LRB-046/1, introduced September 8, 1998, would permit an individual of sound mind, not incapacitated, at least 18 years of age, a resident of Wisconsin, with a terminal disease to request voluntarily, in writing, his or her attending physician to provide medication for the purpose of ending his or her life in a humane and dignified manner. The bill creates a statutory request form for medication and requires that the department of health and family services prepare and provide copies of the request form for distribution to certain facilities, associations, and persons. The request for medication, and the taking of such medication, under this legislation does not, for any purpose, constitute assisted suicide.